A Mystical Trilogy ~ 1

Why are we alive?

Our Search for Meaning

~ Book 1 ~

'Awaken to the meaning of life through this
three-book series of clear, heartfelt spiritual
reflections on spirituality, enlightenment,
and the journey within'.

By Ken Luball

Author's Note

"Why are we alive?" This timeless question lies at the heart of *'Our Search for Meaning' – Book 1*. Written in clear, easily understandable language, these 250 spiritual reflections use metaphor, imagery, and spiritual insight to explore themes of awakening, enlightenment, and the human pursuit of meaning, as it guides readers toward a deeper understanding of life's true purpose. To truly understand each reflection, read only one or two a day and reflect on each one.

My hope writing *'Our Search for Meaning'* was to try to awaken and help others who are awakened more fully understand what enlightenment is so their journey through life may be more fully realized.

As you prepare to begin your search for meaning, do so with an open heart and mind, ready to delve deeper into the mysteries of existence. Let us embark on this spiritual adventure together and, in doing so, discover the answers you are searching for.

Glossary

Asleep – After we are born we are taught how to survive in the world and what success is. We therefore learn to worry only about our own success and survival in the world, rather than to be concerned about others. This results in living in a self-centered world of prejudice, inequity, and endless struggle. Those who fully believe this are asleep, accepting the status quo as the truth.

Awaken – There may come a time in our life when, despite our success in the world, we begin to question the truth of our self-centered learned beliefs, our ego. When this happens the first quiet messages of the spirit, a piece of god present within every life are sensed, beginning us on an enduring journey to discover meaning in our life.

Ego – The ego is everything we learn, believe, and accept is true after we are born, as we learn how to survive in a self-centered world. Its primary concern is what is best for us; it worries little about others. It also attempts to build up our self-esteem by convincing us of our value in the world.

Enlightenment – The complete acceptance of the spiritual path, allowing the spirit's inherent wisdom and unconditional love to be our primary guide in life. With enlightenment, the ego, our self-centered learned beliefs, assumes a secondary role in our life, no longer influencing the direction of our life choices.

<u>Spirit/ Soul/ God / Higher-Self</u> – An ethereal entity accompanying and inextricably connecting every life to another's. Its purpose is to give our lives meaning by sharing its inherent wisdom and unconditional love to help guide our life's choices.

<u>Spirituality</u> – Spirituality is the belief there is a piece of god, a spirit or soul, within every life intimately linking each of us to the other, and, because of this, each life, regardless of our differences, accomplishments, or genus, is important, equal, and connected.

Prologue
Our Search for Meaning

We awaken when we begin
to search for meaning in our
life, sensing the first messages
from our spirit within.
The journey to discover our
true purpose in life is long,
often lonely, and quite
challenging; only a few will
truly find the answers they seek.

It often is not a choice though,
for those who pursue it.
There is a gnawing unrelenting
feeling arising within, no
longer able to be ignored.
This feeling comes from the
spirit, a piece of god, present
within every life.
Our spirit's purpose is to
give our lives meaning by
sharing its inherent wisdom
and unconditional love to
help guide our life's choices.

As these messages become
clearer, we question all the
self-centered choices in life
we had made and everything
we were taught and

believed to be true.
When this happens, we
reevaluate our life choices,
questioning our friendships,
job, beliefs, and everything
else we once thought
gave our life meaning.

With the genuine embrace
of the spiritual path, we realize
little we once thought to be
important really was.
Now, wishing to selflessly
share, without motive or
benefit, our spirit's wisdom
and unconditional love to
benefit others, our search
for meaning will be complete.

Who We Truly Are

Who we truly are has little to do with our appearance; our body is but a shell housing the ego, our self-centered beliefs, and the spirit, present to give our lives meaning by sharing its inherent wisdom and unconditional love to help guide our life's choices. Our value does not lie with the amount of money we make, our job, beliefs, or any other superficial comparisons we may choose to make.

Who we really are lies within us. We will only truly know who we are when we share our spirit's wisdom and love, without motive or benefit, to selflessly help others discover who they truly are as well.

When you look at another, see past their appearance, behind the facade they present to the world, beyond their beliefs and accomplishments in the world. Look to their spirit within each, for that is where the genuine value of a life truly lies.

Why Are We Alive?

If we believe, as many do, the meaning of life is to make money, buy material possessions, have a family, and enjoy the best things life offers, then, though we may be successful, achieving all our goals, we will have lived our life without meaning or purpose. Focusing only on ourself, not selflessly sharing our success with others, our impact on the world, regardless of our accomplishments, will be insignificant.

It is only those who freely share their spirit's innate wisdom and unconditional love with others, irrespective of our many differences, who will discover the genuine reason for our life's journey. Money, material possessions, or anything else found in the world are not necessary to do so. A poor, homeless, uneducated person from a distant land may live a far more purposeful life than one who is wealthy, famous, and has a prestigious job.

Those living their life only for their own benefit, though they and others may believe they have led a meaningful life, have not. Their life will soon be forgotten with the inevitable passage of time. It is only those who sincerely help and share their unconditional love and wisdom, their spirit, with others, without motive or benefit, who will truly discover the genuine reason we are alive.

How Much is a Life Worth?

If we only consider the elements of a human body after it is cremated, one life is worth about a dollar. Is that what a human life is worth? Many people think some lives are more valuable than others, believing those who are wealthy, famous, have a prestigious job, a certain race, ethnicity, religion, are more important than those who are less fortunate, a minority, struggling daily to survive.

Our lives are worth far more than just one dollar. When we start our spiritual journey and awaken, sensing the first messages of our spirit within, we begin to question these self-centered beliefs. The further we travel on the spiritual path, the more we realize little we once believed was true. We now understand an impoverished minority child's life is every bit as worthy and important as the life of someone who is wealthy, famous, or of a different race.

The needless death of even one human being, regardless of their beliefs, appearance, or circumstances in life, affects us all, as their spirit, their essence, is no longer available to share its wisdom and unconditional love with the world. Their life, therefore, as is every life, is invaluable.

Mid-Life Crisis

There may come a time in our life when we begin to question if there is more to life than just what we were told. Though we may be successful, have money, material possessions, a family, there is an uneasy sensation coming from within us, making us question our life choices. This feeling comes from our spirit, present within each life. The spirit helps us discover and fulfill our life's purpose. By following the spiritual path our life will have been lived with genuine meaning and purpose.

Once we awaken, we may never go back to sleep. The only truth is our lives will be changed forever. At this time, we may re-evaluate the job we have, our friendships, and beliefs, as we begin on a spiritual journey. We may change careers, accepting less money, but now helping others through our job. Our friends and family often remain asleep, continuing to live in an illusionary reality, and we may find we now have little in common with them. We therefore may begin to distance ourselves, as we reevaluate everything we once believed to be important.

The midlife crisis is a very challenging time in life, though this awakening may happen at any time in our life. It is a period of reflection as we question everything we have been taught, thought was true, but now begin to realize, had never been. As our crisis deepens, we must make changes in our life. We realize rather than only being concerned for ourselves, we are now equally concerned for everyone else as well. Our only wish now is to help others become successful and discover meaning and purpose in their lives as well.

The End of Life

When we are born, a spirit, a piece of god accompanies each of us. The spirit is the source of divine wisdom and intuition within every life. With our birth, however, the ego, our learned beliefs, is created. Its only concern is what is best for us and our success; it worries little about others. Most blindly follow the self-centered path of the ego, believing success and meaning in life will happen if they make enough money to buy material possessions, have a family, and enjoy the best things life offers.

At the end of life though, something very interesting happens. As we approach death, the ego, which will perish when its body does, loses interest in controlling us. Therefore, it releases its hold on our life at that moment. The messages of the spirit, previously silenced by our dominant ego, can now finally be clearly heard. At this time, we begin to realize everything we once thought important in our life really was not. When we die, just like everyone else, our body will be cremated or buried, and nothing will accompany us. We now realize success in life had little to do with money, material possessions, or anything else we once believed. We finally understand if we had only selflessly shared our success, excess, and unconditional love with others to help them become successful as well, our life would have been lived with genuine meaning and purpose.

We need not wait though until the end of our life to recognize this. There are those who may awaken earlier in their life, sensing the first quiet messages from their spirit within. At that moment, their life changes forever, as they start to make significant changes in their life that will forever alter their future. They begin a quest to find these answers sooner allowing them to seek their life's true destiny.

Behind the Veil

When we are first born we see the world through crystal clear eyes, unimpeded by our self-centered beliefs. Right after our birth, however, the ego, our learned views of the world, is created. From that moment, a veil begins to cover our eyes clouding the beauty of the world around us. The more we accept what we are taught, believing success, happiness, and meaning may be found in the world, the thicker our veil becomes. Many people live their entire life wearing a veil blocking their vision. For some, the veil is so thick, they are almost blind; for others, they see only shadows in the distance. Instead of seeing the crisp clear colors of the world as they are meant to be seen, they see only a dark world of greed, prejudice, inequity; of war, hunger, homelessness.

There are some though who may awaken, sensing the very first messages from their spirit, a piece of god present within each life. The spirit seeks knowledge, wisdom, and ultimate truth about existence. Silenced until now by their overpowering ego, they begin to question if there may be more to life than just what they once believed. As the messages of their spirit become clearer, the veil begins to lift. They begin to realize everything they once thought would allow them to lead a meaningful life may not be true.

With the complete acceptance of the spiritual path, now realizing our life's true purpose is to selflessly share our spirit's wisdom and love to benefit others, we finally are able to remove our veil. We now are able to see the vibrant colors of the trees, oceans, sky, unimpeded by our ego, and the inherent beauty present within all, rather than only the façade and illusion they may present to the world.

A Warning for Humanity

Humanity believes their life is more important than all other forms of life. They even believe the lives of some, due to their differences or accomplishments in the world, are more valuable than others. They have therefore selected an alternative path through life, dictated by the ego, their self-centered beliefs, pursuing only what is best for themselves, rather than for others.

For humanity to survive, they must sense my presence, awaken, and recognize their life is not more important than another's. We are all connected, intimately linked by a piece of god, a spirit within. Only together, sharing our spirit's wisdom and unconditional love with others, will humanity evolve. Apart, as they are now, they are destined to become a footnote in history.

To hear my voice, listen to the silence in between your racing thoughts. Sense my quiet messages within. Follow my thoughtful loving advice, selflessly helping all regardless of differences. This is the genuine purpose of life, the lesson we are alive to understand.

The Human Mosaic

The human mosaic is made up of many different colors when seen together reflect the beauty and love in the world. Most though, choose to see the mosaic, each as a separate hue. This results in prejudice, as we differentiate and judge others by their race, ethnicity, sex, religion, wealth, and in hundreds of other ways. By viewing our world and each other separately, we see only the worst of humanity, resulting in war, hunger, inequity, and the needless struggles from living in a self-centered world.

We need not continue though, to view the world and others this way. Instead, we may choose to see the exquisiteness of the completed mosaic, one where the colors are arranged in a beautiful design. If we do, rather than only seeing the worse in others, we now will see our similarities instead, realizing only together, selflessly sharing our innate wisdom and unconditional love, our spirit with all others, may we all realize life's true potential and understand the genuine reason for our life's journey.

Just like a mosaic, it is when we combine all our differences into a beautiful montage that will we truly understand, it is only by uniting our spirit's wisdom and love with the spirit within all others, the true beauty of life may reveal itself.

The Path to Spirituality

The path to spirituality is exceedingly long, challenging, and arduous. Why anyone would wish to pursue this journey is beyond comprehension. The fact though, is those who choose this path have little choice; there is a gnawing feeling within they may no longer ignore. This awakening begins when the first quiet messages from the spirit begin to be sensed. Though our life may be successful, having money, material possessions, a family, we start to question if there may be more to life, a further purpose we must pursue.

At this point, we begin to reevaluate our choices in life. As the messages from our spirit become more prominent, our friendships, job, beliefs about the world, are all challenged. Though we are changing, we continue to live in a self-centered world, where our friends and family often remain asleep, continuing to live in an illusional world they still believe is real.

Once we awaken, we may never go back to sleep. We begin to adopt the spiritual path, wishing to selflessly share our excess, wisdom, and unconditional love now, our spirit, to help those in need. There are few questions left now as we understand the genuine meaning of life never had anything to do with what we once believed. Rather, it is to selflessly help others realize the genuine intent of their life as well.

Listen to the Silence

Before we are born, a spirit, a piece of god joins a new life. Its purpose is to guide our life with its wisdom and unconditional love. At this time all we hear is silence. With our very first breath though, we arrive into a bright, loud, chaotic world of endless noise. Even if we manage to find a little silence during our life, our mind continues to endlessly race with thoughts of yesterday, today, and tomorrow. Our life is so busy, there simply is no time left for silence. We learn how to become successful and live a meaningful life in a self-centered world, being taught money, material possessions, family, will allow us to achieve our goals. Those who believe this remain asleep, living in an illusionary matrix they believe is real.

If we listen intently enough though, to the silence in between our racing thoughts, we may sense a quiet message within. This message is from our spirit, awakening us to the possibility our definition of success and meaning may be flawed. As the messages from our spirit become clearer, the periods of silence become longer. We begin to realize everything we were told, believing it would make our life meaningful and successful, was untrue. It was all fiction, created by the self-serving ego, our learned beliefs, to have us pursue a false path through life.

We were always meant to follow the spiritual path, one that selflessly shares our spirit's unconditional love and wisdom with others, so everyone in life, regardless of our differences, would be able to succeed and live a meaningful life as well. With the complete acceptance of the spiritual path, the silence endures, as the lessons we are born to understand, the genuine meaning of our life's journey, are understood.

The Dream

After we are born, our beliefs, prejudices, and ideas are formed, as we learn about the self-centered world we are living in. We are taught success is making money, allowing us to buy material possessions, have a family, and enjoy the best things life offers. When we accept and believe all we are taught we remain asleep, dreaming our life is successful and worthwhile. Often, we never wake from our slumber, approaching death not even realizing we were ever asleep. Though we may have led a successful life, had wealth, fame, prestige, it was all an illusion, a dream, fabricated by the ego, our learned beliefs, to have us believe it was real; it never was.

Some may begin to awaken from their sleep, sensing the first messages from their spirit within. They start to wonder if there may be more to life than just what they learned. As they further awaken from their dream, they begin to realize their life will never be truly successful if they focus only on themselves.

The purpose of life is to completely wake from our slumber, end our illusionary dream, realizing the genuine reason we are alive is to help everyone, regardless of our differences, find success, purpose, and meaning in their life as well.

Waking Up Is Hard To Do

Before we are born we are enlightened, knowing there is a spirit, a piece of god present within not only us, but every life as well. The spirit is the guiding wisdom and truth within. But with our first breath, the ego, our learned beliefs, is created. And with the creation of the ego and the acceptance of its self-centered beliefs, we begin to fall asleep. The more we believe what we are taught, the deeper our slumber will be.

There may come a time in our life though, very often around middle age, although it could happen anytime, where we start to sense an uneasy feeling within. This feeling comes from our spirit trying to get our attention to let us know we are following the wrong path through life. Once this sensation begins, it will not go away; our life will change forever. We have no choice but to pursue it; we have awoken.

As the messages of our spirit become clearer, we begin to re-evaluate our life. We reconsider our job, friendships, perhaps even our marriage, as many people we know remain asleep, still believing everything they learned in life is true. We therefore may begin to distance ourself from them as the things important to them no longer have meaning to us. With the acceptance of the spiritual path, selflessly sharing our spirit's wisdom and love to help others, our life will be forever changed. Understanding every life, regardless of our differences, accomplishments, or genus, each with a piece of god within, is equally important, we now wish to help others realize this as well.

Waking up is very hard to do. The journey as we challenge all our self-centered beliefs, slowly realizing they were not true, is extremely difficult. But when we fully wake, we will have learned the lesson we are alive to understand.

Imagine God is a Star

Imagine god is a star representing warmth, light, universal wisdom, and unconditional love. Next imagine the rays of the star, which are part of god, represent the spirit or a piece of god. As the rays travel through the dark universe, they reach a planet. Everything the rays touch are therefore infused with a piece of god. On our planet, it matters not if the rays touch mountains, rivers, rocks, flowers, trees, people, animals, each is infused with the spirit of god.

A piece of god therefore resides within not only each of us, but within everything the rays of the star infuse with its light as well, intimately joining each to the other. Though we are all different, we are linked by the piece of god within each of us. The meaning of life is to selflessly share our light, warmth, wisdom, and love with all others to help them discover their light within as well.

God does not see differences. Every life is inextricably connected by the spirit. Each, therefore, regardless of our differences, accomplishments, or genus, infused with the rays of the star, is equal; no one life is, or every has been better, or more important than another's. When we die, our spirit will then return to its star, until it will join a new life when its rays leave their source, infusing another with a piece of god once again.

The Spiritual Journey

The spirit is the source of divine wisdom and intuition within us. Following its path through life is the reason we are alive.

With our first breath, however, the ego, our learned beliefs, is created. The result of believing all we are taught is concern only for ourselves, rather than others. The more we accept what we learn, the further from the spiritual path we will drift. We therefore ignore the prejudice, inequity, and innumerable struggles of others, focusing only on our own success and happiness in life instead.

We awaken when the first messages from our spirit begin to be sensed. Until now, its voice had been silenced by our overpowering ego. An uneasy sensation comes from deep within; a feeling we can no longer ignore. It questions our self-centered beliefs, wishing us to reevaluate everything we believe to be true. Though we may be successful in life, it will not inhibit this feeling of unease. Eventually, we have no choice but to challenge our beliefs, as we begin to search for genuine meaning in our life.

As the spiritual messages become more prevalent, our life begins to change significantly; we reevaluate our friendships, job, convictions. Instead of only being concerned for ourselves, we now wish to help others as well. As we remain on this new path through life, the spirit eventually becomes our primary guide, allowing us once more to embrace the loving spiritual path we were always meant to follow.

Our Human Limitations

Before we are born we are spirit, each possessing a piece of god present within every life. The spirit helps us discover and fulfill our life's purpose.

With our first breath, though, the ego, our self-centered beliefs, is created, inhibiting our view of life. The more we accept our learned beliefs, the more limited our life will be. Success, wealth, having a prestigious job, will not alleviate our human limitations. They will not abate until we once again remember who we truly are: we are spirit.

We awaken when we sense the first messages from our spirit within, questioning the truth of all we learned. The more we realize these beliefs are untrue, the clearer the messages from our spirit become. Enlightenment is the total acceptance of the spiritual path through life, allowing the spirit to become our primary guide in life. With this realization, our human limitations mitigate as the genuine purpose of our life's journey, to selflessly share our spirit's wisdom and love to help others, now becomes evident.

Open Your Eyes

Before we take our first breath and are exposed to the chaos and noise of the world, our eyes are wide open. A spirit, a piece of god is already present within every life. Its purpose is to transcend ignorance and reach divine understanding. By selflessly sharing our spirit's wisdom and love to benefit others, we will have learned the lesson we are alive to understand.

With our first breath, though, the ego, our learned beliefs, is created. As we begin to accept the self-centered views of the world, our eyes start to close. The more we believe everything we learn in life is true, the less we are able to see. By the time many become adults, though their eyes appear open, they are totally glazed over, completely blind to the genuine purpose of life.

There may come a time in our life, though, when we begin to sense the first quiet messages from our spirit within, questioning the truth of what we were taught. With this awakening, our eyes begin to reopen. As our spirit's messages become clearer, we begin to understand everything we learned about life, all of our self-centered learned beliefs, were not true. Now when we see another, instead of seeing just their race, ethnicity, accomplishments in the world, we no longer judge them by what we see.

With the complete acceptance of the spiritual path, our eyes are wide open once again. We now are able to see all others beyond their exterior, the outer shell, the facade they present to the world, to who they truly are. They are spirit, just as we and all others are, alive to selflessly share our wisdom and love, to help others understand this as well.

We Are Born Enlightened

We are born enlightened; a spirit, a piece of god is already present within every life. The spirit is the guiding wisdom and truth present within every life. With our birth, however, the ego, our self-centered beliefs, is created. For many, the ego dominates their life, becoming their primary guide, silencing the messages from their spirit within.

Many therefore believe money, allowing them to buy material possessions and enjoy the best things life may offer, will determine if their life is successful. Many go through their entire life never sensing their spirit's messages. And though they may live to an old age, lead a successful life, they will die without ever discovering their life's true purpose.

Others though, may awaken during their life, sensing the first quiet messages from their spirit within, questioning if there may be more to life than money. As the messages become more prominent, they begin to reassess their life, now wishing to selflessly help others become successful as well.

With the acceptance of the loving spiritual path, allowing the spirit rather than the ego to be our primary guide in life, we begin in earnest our journey back toward enlightenment. It is ironic; we are born enlightened, then spend the rest of our life trying to return to that moment we once knew, just before we took our first breath.

What is Spirituality?

Spirituality is quite different from religion. Religion, when it first began, was a noble undertaking. Wishing to embrace god, religion shared ideas such as love, morality, the difference between good and evil, among many other idealistic thoughts with their worshipers. But over time, most religions adopted humanity's self-centered interpretations of the meaning of these terms, mitigating their influence on others.

Spirituality is the belief there is a piece of god, a spirit or soul, within every life, and because of this, each life is important, equal, and connected. The spirit is present in all life, be it human, animals, plants; it links every life together. Spirituality desires what is best for everyone, rather than just the individual. It realizes to succeed in the world and live a life of true meaning and purpose, we must all work together; that no one life, regardless of our differences or accomplishments, is or ever has been, more important than another's.

Success in life has little to do with money or material possessions. Rather it may only be achieved by selflessly helping each other, sharing our unconditional love and excess, so everyone may succeed in life together.

We Are All Ohana (Family)

In Hawaii, the word ohana means family. This includes those closest to us, our neighbors, those who look or believe differently, and even complete strangers. If anyone who is ohana needs help, it is gladly given without question or reason. This definition of family aligns extraordinarily well with enlightenment, for enlightenment is selflessly sharing our spirit's inherent wisdom and unconditional love with all others, regardless of our differences, to selflessly help those in need. That is the meaning of life, the lesson we are alive to learn.

The world in which we live, however, has a very different definition of family, believing only our nuclear family, consisting of parents, children, grandparents, are family; all others, though some may be friends, are simply acquaintances or strangers. Our concern therefore is only for ourselves and those closest to us, worrying little for anyone else. This is the cause of indifference, inequity, and many of humanity's self-inflicted challenges and beliefs, where a few do well, while most endlessly struggle to survive.

After we awaken, sensing the first quiet messages from our spirit within, we begin to understand every person, even those we do not know, is intimately connected, linked by a spirit, a piece of god present within each of us. With this understanding, we now realize it matters not if someone is family, different from us, or complete strangers; we truly are all ohana, family, related, brothers and sisters, alive to selflessly help everyone succeed, find love, purpose, and meaning in their life as well.

A Long and Winding Road

With our birth, the ego, our learned beliefs, is created. The ego's only concern is what is best for us; it worries little about others. As we are socialized to accept the self-centered beliefs of the world, many adopt its views, prejudices, and fears. They therefore remain asleep, their life dictated by their blind obedience to their egoistic beliefs. This obedience is the cause of many of humanity's self-inflicted problems and harmful emotions.

There are some who awaken from their slumber though, as the first messages from their spirit within are sensed, questioning if what they were taught about life is true. Though they may be successful, they begin to wonder if there is more to life than making money, having material possessions, and enjoying the many pleasures life offers.

Though they may have awoken, the path to enlightenment is quite long and challenging, as we begin to drift away from our friends and family who often remain asleep. As the messages of our spirit become clearer, we begin to understand everything we once believed to be true, was not. We now realize every life, each having a spirit, a piece of god within, regardless of our differences or accomplishments, is equally important, and rather than only being worried about ourselves, we are now concerned for others as well.

We are all on this journey of life together and only together, by sharing our spirit's inherent wisdom and unconditional love to selflessly help each other, will our life have genuine purpose and meaning.

What is a Spiritual Awakening?

Before we are first born, we know only one emotion: unconditional love. This emotion arises from our spirit, present within every life; its purpose is to transcend ignorance and reach divine understanding. When we are born though, the ego, our learned beliefs, is created as well. Though the ego is important to help us survive in the world, its only concern is what is best for us; it worries little for anyone else.

Many people believe what they are taught about life, thinking success is making money, having material possessions, a family, and doing the best things life has to offer. The result of this fallacy is a self-centered world of endless struggle, prejudice, and inequity. Those who believe what they were taught, though they may be successful and achieve all their goals, go through their life asleep, never realizing their true purpose in life.

There may come a time in our life though, when we begin to question if what we learned was true; that perhaps there is more to life, a deeper purpose. These thoughts arise from our spirit, awakening us to life's genuine possibilities. The messages we receive are about selflessly helping all others, and the equal importance of every life. Once we awaken, we may never go back to sleep, as we begin to reevaluate our entire life, determined now to make our life's journey truly meaningful and worthwhile.

Life's Illusions

What is real and what is an illusion? Those who remain asleep accept everything they learn is real. They believe to be happy and live a successful meaningful life, they must make money, have material possessions, a family, and do the best things life offers. Believing this, though they may accomplish all their goals, they will have lived their life without meaning or purpose, chasing an illusion, a dream which was never attainable in a self-centered world.

Almost everything we learn in life is an illusion, based on a false narrative created by the ego, our learned beliefs. What is real is our spirit, the piece of god accompanying each of us on our life's journey. We awaken when we first sense its presence within, beginning us on an irreversible path of self-discovery. We start to question if what we learned about finding success and meaning in the world was true. We become enlightened when we realize none of it was; it was all a mirage, an illusion, masking our genuine purpose in life: to allow our spirit to guide our life with its inherent wisdom and unconditional love, so we may selflessly share its wisdom and love to help others realize this as well.

The Spirit and the Ego

Within each person is both a spirit and an ego, accompanying them throughout their life. The spirit is a piece of god; its purpose is to dissolve separation and experience oneness with all beings. The ego is created with our first breath; it is everything we are taught and believe to be true as we learn to accept the self-centered traditions and beliefs of the world. The spirit and the ego each compete for dominance throughout our life.

The ego's only concern is us; it worries little for others. Most in the world follow this path through life, accepting the many challenges, difficulties, and struggles resulting from choosing the ego as their primary guide. War, hunger, homelessness; greed, prejudice, inequity, are but a few of hundreds of problems and harmful emotions resulting from living in such a world. When the ego dominates our life, the quiet messages of our spirit within are subdued.

There may come a time in our life though, when we awaken, as the first muffled messages of our spirit are sensed. This moment ushers in a time of great change, as we begin to reevaluate our life and the truth of what we once believed. We reassess our definition of success, happiness, and what is truly important. As the messages from the spirit become more prominent, we may change our job, reevaluate our friendships, wishing now to selflessly help others, instead of only worrying about ourselves. With this realization, our spirit now becomes our primary guide in life, allowing us to begin in earnest our journey toward enlightenment.

The Three Stages of Enlightenment

The first stage of enlightenment is being asleep. It begins when we are born as we learn what is expected of us and how to survive in a self-centered world. Those who go through their entire life believing what they were taught is true remain asleep. When they approach death, though they may have led a successful life, it will have lived without purpose or meaning.

The second stage of enlightenment is awakening. Awakening begins when we start to sense the first quiet messages from our spirit within, questioning if there may be more to life than what we were told. The spirit is a piece of god, our higher-self, accompanying every life. Its intention is to guide our lives with its inherent wisdom and unconditional love.

The third stage of enlightenment is enlightenment. With the complete acceptance of the spiritual path through life, we realize our genuine purpose in life is to selflessly share our spirit's wisdom and love to help others discover their true purpose in life as well.

The Tree of Life

Picture a large, majestic, old tree with roots reaching deep into the earth. Its roots absorb water and nourishment, its large, magnificent trunk is topped by many branches full of leaves. Now, imagine the trunk of the tree is our planet. The thicker branches of the tree represent the larger divisions in the world and the smaller branches are those divisions further separated. For example, let's consider one thick branch represents religion, with its smaller branches being individual beliefs such as Buddhist, Hindu, Christian. This is true for the other thick branches for ethnicity, race, and hundreds of other divisions in the world as well.

Next, imagine each leaf is a single person. One leaf alone will not be sufficient to absorb enough CO_2, release enough O_2, offer enough shade for the animals seeking refuge from the summer heat or provide enough nourishment when it falls before winter solstice for its roots to absorb. If we put all the leaves together on one branch, though it will help a little more, it will still not be sufficient to accomplish all it must do.

Let's compare humanity to the leaves of the tree and to the tree itself. We live in a self-centered world encouraging us to be concerned only for ourselves. Our one leaf, though it may successfully survive until winter, alone it will not provide enough nourishment for the soul and soon will be forgotten. Its life, when it finally falls before winter solstice, will have been led without purpose or meaning. The same may be said for all of the leaves on all of the branches of the tree.

Only when we unite all the branches together, each full of leaves, will the tree be able to accomplish its purpose. Not only will it be able to absorb enough carbon dioxide, release enough oxygen into our atmosphere, but it will also provide enough shade for refuge for all the animals and sufficient nourishment for the roots when its leaves fall before winter. Doing so, the tree trunk, our planet, will survive, allowing it, and all who grace its presence, to thrive.

Many Paths, One Destination

We each follow our own unique path. We may be wealthy or poor, Christian or Buddhist, Hispanic or Asian, or any of hundreds of other differences that may influence our lives. Regardless of the circumstances in our life though, we all have the same destination: to become one with our higher-self, our spirit, the piece of god accompanying each of us through our life's journey. Selflessly sharing our spirit's inherent wisdom and unconditional love to help others, without motive or benefit, is the genuine purpose of our life's journey, our destination.

Though we each experience life differently, anyone, *despite* their life challenges, may reach the final destination. It matters not our religion, wealth, race, ethnicity, sex, or any other differences we may have. The challenge obstructing our path is the acceptance of our self-centered learned beliefs, silencing the messages our spirit desperately wishes to share with us. Those who do not hear these messages, though they may achieve success in their life, never find the true path they are meant to pursue or discover genuine meaning in their life.

We awaken when we first sense the soft muffled messages from our spirit within, as we begin to question if everything we were taught was true. As these messages become clearer, we begin to understand they were not. With the total acceptance of the spiritual path, we share our spirit's wisdom and love, allowing our destination to be approached. There is a feeling of extraordinary inner peace and boundless love, as we now wish to help others reach their destination as well.

The Root of All Problems

Before we are born, we are spirit, having a piece of god present within, intimately linking each of us to the other. Our spirit's purpose is to give our lives meaning by sharing its inherent wisdom and unconditional love to help guide our life's choices.

The root of all of problems begin with our first breath, when the ego, our learned beliefs, is created. Our ego's only concern is us, worrying little about others. By accepting what we are taught, we learn success is making money, having material possessions, a family, enjoying life. This belief is the cause of many of humanity's self-inflicted problems and harmful emotions. War, hunger, prejudice, inequity, are but a few of hundreds of challenges caused by embracing this self-centered view of life.

Though we know others are suffering, needlessly dying from starvation, senseless violence, indifference, we believe there is little we may do to change this. Most, therefore, simply accept these hardships as a normal part of life. The root of all problems is the dominance of the ego, silencing the loving messages of our spirit within.

These problems may only begin to mitigate when we awaken, sensing the first quiet messages from our spirit. As our spirit's messages become more prominent, our ego assumes a secondary quieter role. With this reversal, we start to realize everything we had learned about success, happiness, and meaning, was not true; that the genuine purpose of our life's journey is to selflessly share our spirit's wisdom and love so all others may find success, happiness, and meaning in their life as well.

Humanity's Arrogance

Humanity believes it is the most important species in the world. They think, since they are more intelligent, they are superior to all other forms of life and the planet we inhabit; therefore, they may treat each with disdain. There are those who even believe some people are more important, more deserving than others, due to their race, ethnicity, beliefs, wealth, or any of hundreds of other comparisons that differentiate us from each other. This arrogance is the cause of many man-made challenges and harmful beliefs plaguing the world both today and throughout history.

Humanity though, has never been better than any other form of life or each other. Each, infused with a spirit, a piece of god within, inextricably connects us all together. Every life, regardless of our differences or genus, is equally important. Each therefore, is as deserving as another. And our planet, which sustains us all, is the most crucial of all. Each must be treated with respect and unconditional love. Only together, realizing the importance and symbiotic relationship of each, will we all survive and may humanity's arrogance transform to humility, allowing our planet and all who inhabit it to thrive.

When Death Approaches

When we are born, the ego, our learned beliefs, is created. The ego is self-centered, worried only for what is best for us; it has little concern for anyone else. It teaches us we will find happiness, success, and meaning in the world by making money, having material possessions, a family, and enjoying the best things money allows us to do. The result of living in such a world are greed, prejudice, inequity, and many of humanity's problems caused by following this self-centered path through life.

When we approach death though, an interesting thing happens. Our ego realizes that it, along with our body, will perish. It therefore releases its hold on our life. At that time, without the ego's dominance, we begin to sense our spirit, a piece of god present within every life. Its voice had been muted until now by our overpowering ego. Our spirit tells us happiness, success, and meaning could never be found in the world, as we believed. It must first be found within, by embracing the inherent wisdom and unconditional love of the spirit, then selflessly sharing its wisdom and love to help others find happiness, success, and meaning in their lives as well.

If this happens only as death approaches, it is too late for most. Though they may have led a successful life, accomplished all their goals, had wealth, when they die, their life will have been lived without meaning or purpose.

We need not wait though, until we approach death. It is possible to awaken earlier in life, sensing the first loving messages from our spirit within. To do so, sit silently, listen intently to the quiet whispers in between your thoughts, then follow the messages you hear.

We Are Immortal

As we are growing up, we are indoctrinated into a self-centered world. We learn to survive and succeed in this world we must make money. Believing this, though we may become successful and wealthy, if it only benefits us and not others, our life will have been led without meaning or purpose. And though we may have lived a good life and achieved all our goals, if we did not selflessly share our excess and success with others, when we die, we will soon be forgotten, continuing only in the memory of our family and a few close friends.

Within each person though, is also a spirit, a piece of god accompanying each of us throughout our life. The spirit guides us toward spiritual awakening and higher understanding. It matters not our differences, accomplishments, or if another is a stranger, understanding every life is equally important. With the acceptance of the spiritual path through life, the number of people our spirit intimately connects with goes far beyond just our family and friends.

When we freely share our love and excess, without motive or benefit, our spirit joins with the spirit of another. When we die, therefore, part of our spirit will continue to live on in the spirit of all the people we have influenced and selflessly helped in our life. In turn, our spirit, which is now integrated with the spirit of those we helped, will be shared with those they help as well, allowing our spirit to be immortal and our life to have been lived with genuine meaning and purpose.

A Total Eclipse of the Sun

Imagine the sun shining its light on a clear summer day. Its light is unwavering, unobstructed by clouds above. Similar to the sun, before we are born, the purpose of our life's journey is completely clear as well. It is to follow the guidance of our spirit, a piece of god present within each life, selflessly sharing its inherent wisdom and unconditional love with others. The spirit recognizes no distinctions, realizing every life, each having a piece of god within, is equally important and that, only together, sharing our spirit's wisdom and love with each other, will all our lives have meaning.

After we are born though, the ego, our learned beliefs, is created. Our ego cares little about others; its focus is only on what is best for us. We are taught the purpose of life is to get a well-paying job allowing us to have material possessions, a family, and enjoy life's many pleasures. The eclipse of the sun begins with our acceptance of these self-centered beliefs. The more we believe what we are taught, the greater the eclipse of the sun will be, blocking the once pristine bright light we knew before we were born. As the light of the sun begins to disappear, the problems of the world accentuate. For many, fully believing this view of life, the eclipse of the sun is total, its light only seen around its periphery.

There may come a time in our life, though, when the total eclipse of the sun starts to fade as the moon begins to move past the sun's core. With this awakening, we sense the first messages from our spirit within; small cracks in our ego's dominance begin to form, attempting to let us know everything we learned in life may not be true. As the moon moves further away from the center of the sun, allowing its light to be more visible, we begin to re-evaluate our friendships, job, and beliefs, as many people in our life remain asleep.

When the eclipse ends and the moon has fully passed the sun's orbit, we once again are able to see the bright shining light we once knew before we were born. We now realize everything we once believed to be true, never was; rather it was meant to challenge our life choices. We once again understand the genuine purpose of life, the lesson we are alive to learn, is to embrace the guidance of our loving spirit, selflessly sharing its wisdom and love, without motive or benefit, with all others, to help them understand their true purpose in life as well.

There Are Only Two Paths Through Life

Though life is mystifying and complex, there are only two possible paths we may take: the self-centered path of the ego, our learned beliefs, or the path of the spirit, present within every life to help us discover and fulfill our life's purpose. Whichever path primarily guides our life will determine if we find genuine meaning, happiness, and love during our life's journey.

The ego is the path most follow. Its self-serving agenda is the cause of most of humanity's self-inflicted challenges and harmful behaviors. War, hunger, homelessness; greed, prejudice, inequity, are but a few of hundreds of problems resulting from living in such a world. Success is defined as having money, material possessions, enjoying life. Though we may achieve all our goals, our life will have been led without purpose or meaning.

The spirit intimately links every life together. Unlike the ego, the spirit's concern is for everyone. Its goal is to help others succeed in their lives as well. Money, material possessions, prestige, are not necessary to achieve this goal. Anyone, regardless of our differences, accomplishments, or circumstances in life may live a successful life. To do so, open your heart, selflessly share your wisdom and love, your spirit with others, so they too may find meaning, happiness, and love in their lives as well.

Are Animals Sentient?

Gaze into the eyes of an animal. Behind those eyes, beyond what we see, is a spirit, a soul, a piece of god, no different than the spirit within each person and every other form of life as well. If you look deeply enough, you will see, past the exterior and our self-centered learned beliefs, there is a spirit present not only within each of us, but within all animals as well.

The spirit is present to provide meaning to our lives by sharing its wisdom and unconditional love to benefit others. It intimately links each of us to the other and to the universe itself. Regardless of our differences, achievements, or genus, we are all the same, each with a piece of god within, and must selflessly help others in their time of need. Only when humanity truly understands this will they spiritually evolve, allowing our planet and all who inhabit it, to live in a world of love, hope, and peace, rather than to continue to live in a world of hate, indifference, and endless war.

The Appearance of Meaning

Learning how to survive in the world, most people believe
everything they were taught. They therefore seek meaning through
their job, family, material possessions, religion, and in other ways.
Meaning found in a self-centered world though, is an illusion.
Though we may achieve our goals, if we don't selflessly share our
success, love, and excess with others, our life will have been lived
without meaning or purpose.

Genuine meaning may only be found by embracing the spiritual path
through life. Our spirit is the transcendent aspect of human
awareness that connects to something greater than the self. When we
selflessly join our spirit with others, uniting our purpose as one, we
may find meaning not only in the world, but uncover the genuine
meaning of our life's journey as well.

With Awakening Everything Changes

Before we are born, a spirit, a piece of god joins every life. Our spirit's purpose is to dissolve separation and experience oneness with all beings. With our birth, though, the ego, our learned beliefs, is created. The ego's only concern is what is best for us; it worries little about others.

Most follow the self-centered beliefs of the ego, concerned only about themselves. When the ego is dominant, it silences the messages of the spirit within. Those who never hear those messages, despite their accomplishments or success in life, live their life oblivious to the lessons they are born to understand.

There may come a time in our life though, we awaken, sensing the first quiet messages from our spirit within. Once we awaken, we may never go back to sleep. We have no choice but to pursue a new path, wondering if there is more to life than what we were told. We begin to question and re-evaluate everything in our life, including our job, relationships, beliefs.

As our spirit's messages become more prominent we now realize only together, selflessly helping each other, may we all succeed and live a life of genuine purpose and meaning.

Is It Too Late to Change the World?

We live in a world of inequity, greed, prejudice; of war, hunger, homelessness. A world where many people are unhappy, stressed, struggling daily to survive. This, and many other man-made problems and harmful emotions are the result of living in a self-centered world, concerned only for what is best for us, rather than for others. Most believe these things are a normal part of life, but they need not be.

We have the technology now to end hunger, homelessness, climate change, and many of humanity's greatest challenges. We have the ability now to end indifference, greed, prejudice, and all of mankind's harmful emotions. By adopting the spiritual path through life, selflessly sharing our innate wisdom and unconditional love, our spirit with each other, we may change the world now.

Humanity has a choice to make, but it will take a monumental shift of consciousness, a spiritual revolution; one where what is best for everyone and our planet itself, takes precedence over what is best only for ourselves or the few. The change must first begin within each of us, realizing our genuine purpose in life is to embrace the wisdom and loving messages of our spirit within, then share them, without motive or benefit, with the world. It is not too late to do this, but time for change is rapidly vanishing. If we do nothing, the choice may be made for us.

The Illusion of Happiness

The illusion of happiness begins when we are first born, learning how to be successful and find happiness in a self-centered world. We are told we must get a good job, make money, have material possessions, a family, enjoy life's many pleasures to live a happy, successful life.

We awaken when, though we may have achieved all our goals, happiness continue to elude us; we begin to wonder if perhaps there may be more to life. An uneasy feeling starts to emerge suggesting something is missing. This feeling arises from our spirit, a piece of god present within every life.

True happiness and success may not be found in the world. They must first be discovered within, then our spirit's innate wisdom and unconditional love must be selflessly shared to help others find success and happiness in their lives as well.

Choosing Love Over Fear

We each have a choice how we are going to live our life. We may choose to live our life either with love or fear. Most choose the latter, living their life in fear, accepting the self-centered beliefs of the world, concerned only for what is best for themselves rather than others. The result of living in such a world is war, inequity, prejudice, hunger, homelessness, and many of humanity's self-inflicted problems and harmful emotions.

We, however, may choose to live our life with love instead by embracing the innate wisdom and unconditional love present within every life. When we live our life with love, we share our love unconditionally, selflessly with all others. Instead of being concerned only for ourselves, we are now equally worried about everyone else as well. When we look at another, we do not see their race, ethnicity, wealth, or any other differences between us. Instead, we only see a fellow spiritual traveler, each alive to learn the messages our spirit desperately wishes to share with us: to choose love over fear.

What Happens After You Awaken?

We are born awakened, enlightened, each with a spirit, a piece of god within, present to share its innate wisdom and unconditional love allowing us to live a life of genuine meaning and purpose. With our birth, however, the ego, our learned beliefs, is created. As we are indoctrinated into society, our opinions, beliefs, and prejudices are formed. Living in a self-centered world, we are taught success is defined as having money, material possessions, amongst other things, allowing us to enjoy the best things life offers. For most, their ego dominates their life, muting the messages of their loving spirit within.

There may come a time for some though, even if they are successful, they begin to sense an uneasy feeling within. This awakening comes from their spirit, as its first messages are recognized. Once they awaken, they may never go back to sleep; everything in their life will change forever. Many of their relationships with friends and family may begin to fade; though we are changing, others often remain asleep, still believing success may be found in the world. They may even change jobs, be willing to take less money, so their job will be more fulfilling. As they further divest themself of many of their self-centered beliefs they now wish to selflessly help others become successful, rather than only worrying about their own success.

Enlightenment is the complete acceptance of the spiritual path through life. Though few will achieve this in their lifetime, it is the journey we are alive to experience.

We Are Stronger Together

After we are born, the ego, our learned beliefs, is created, teaching us to worry only about our own success and happiness in life, even if it may harm or cause undue struggle for others. Much of the world believe what they are taught, serving only to divide, rather than unite us. It is the cause of prejudice, greed, inequity; of war, hunger, homelessness, and many of humanity's harmful emotions and self-inflicted challenges in the world.

Though we may achieve our goals in life, have money, material possessions, a family, our life may yet feel unfulfilled. With this feeling, arising from the spirit, our higher-self within, we begin to reevaluate our beliefs. Once we awaken, everything in our life will change. We start to redefine our definition of success and happiness. We now understand that only by helping others find success and happiness in their lives as well will our life have been lived with genuine purpose and meaning.

Together, selflessly helping each other, we all become stronger, helping to mitigate many of humanity's hardships resulting from living in a self-centered world. Apart, continuing to follow the status quo, we will leave our children a world of unimaginable struggle and endless challenges.

Our True Path in Life

Humanity believes, since they are more intelligent, their lives are more important than all other forms of life and the planet that sustains them. It therefore has the right to abuse and needlessly kill lower lifeforms and destroy our planet with impunity. They even believe the lives of some people, because of their race, sex, religion, wealth, or any of hundreds of other differences, are better, more significant than others who are different from them.

This is not what the human condition truly is though. Rather, it is the result of accepting everything we are taught about how to survive in a self-centered world. Though humanity has significantly evolved technologically over the past centuries, spiritually, it has not. The genuine human condition involves following the spiritual path, realizing only by selflessly sharing our excess, innate wisdom, and unconditional love, our spirit, with others, will the authentic human condition reveal itself. With this awareness comes the understanding no one life, regardless of our differences or genus, is or ever has been better, more important than another's, and only together, respecting every life and our planet itself, will our human condition allow us all to thrive and live a life of genuine meaning and purpose.

Spiritual Karma

Karma is when the universe has a response to something we do. There are some people who appear to get away with everything, often taking advantage of others, causing them harm with their words, actions, or deeds. They seem to suffer no consequences for the pain they have caused. When they near death though, as the ego, their learned beliefs, releases its hold on their life, they will relive all the harm and pain they caused to others, clearly re-experiencing every detail before their passing.

Spiritual debt occurs when we do or say anything contrary to the spiritual path in life we are meant to follow. Our true purpose in life is to reunite with our spirit, the piece of god present within every life, then selflessly share its inherent wisdom and unconditional love to help others realize this is their purpose in life as well. This is the meaning of life, the lesson we are here to learn.

Spiritual karma will continue to accrue every day we are alive until the harm is corrected by us doing the right thing. If we do not, the spiritual debt will then be paid in full when death approaches, as we relive every moment we needlessly caused harm to another.

What is a Successful Life?

After we are born we are taught what success is. We learn to be successful we must get a good education, well-paying job, make enough money to allow us to buy a house, have material possessions, a family, and do all the best things life offers. We believe if we do all these things we will have lived a very successful life.

Is that what success truly is though? When we approach death, many review their life's choices. They may find at that time they have regrets, realizing many of the things they once thought important, truly were not. When death is imminent, the ego, our learned beliefs, will perish when its body does. Its influence therefore wanes at this time and the spirit, a piece of god present within every life, becomes our primary messenger.

Now, clearly hearing our spirit's messages, we understand success in life had little to do with what we accomplished in the world; money, material possessions, or anything else we once believed would bring us true happiness and meaning, never could do so. If our success was not selflessly shared to help others succeed as well, we now realize our life was not a success; instead, it was lived without purpose or meaning.

The genuine meaning of life is to selflessly share our spirit's wisdom and unconditional love, regardless of our differences, with others. If we do, though we may have been poor, struggled throughout our life, we will have lived a very successful life.

What are the Lessons We are Alive to Learn?

After we are born, we are taught how to survive in a self-centered world. We learn to find happiness, meaning, and success in our life we must get a good job, have material possessions, a family, and make enough money to be able to enjoy life's many pleasures. Is this the lesson we are alive to learn?

Humanity believes because it is the most intelligent and dominant species on our planet they have a right to abuse and disrespect, not only other forms of life, but our planet, and each other as well. They therefore needlessly kill animals, trees, and other forms of life, though there are now alternative food sources for sustenance and materials for heat and to build homes. They senselessly kill each other in wars due to the greed of the few and powerful, and are destroying our planet, endlessly poisoning its land, air, and water, though we have the ability to mitigate this today.

In spirituality, there is a belief there are many other lessons, quite contrary to what we were taught, that we are meant to learn as well. We discover there is a spirit, a piece of god present within every life. The spirit's purpose is to seek knowledge, wisdom, and ultimate truth about existence. There is also a realization every life, regardless of our differences or genus, each having a spirit within, is equally important. Only together, realizing the symbiotic relationship of every life to each other's, may we all not only survive, but also learn the genuine lessons we are alive to understand as well.

The Four Dimensions of the Spirit

A spirit is a piece of god, our higher-self, present within every life; its purpose is to give our lives meaning, inextricably linking each life to another's. It matters not our differences or genus; each life has a spirit within. The spirit embodies wisdom and unconditional love meant to be selflessly shared with others, each with a spirit within as well.

To understand the four dimensions of the spirit, imagine god is a star. The first dimension of the spirit are the rays of light and warmth emitted from the star. Each ray symbolizes a part of god, as its rays travel through an endless universe. The second dimension of the spirit happens when the rays of light reach a planet. Everything this light touches, whether it be mountains, streams, animals, plants, people, are now infused with the spirit.

The third dimension of the spirit are in higher forms of life, such as animals and human beings. Since the light touches every person, we each have a piece of god within as well. Only by following the spiritual path through life, accepting its messages by selflessly sharing our spirit's innate wisdom and unconditional love with the spirit within all others, may our life have genuine meaning and purpose.

The last dimension of the spirit happens when we die. Though our body and ego, our learned beliefs, will perish, our spirit is immortal, returning to the star it first came from, until its rays of light once again are emitted into the vastness of the universe.

We Must Open Our Eyes

From the moment we are born, we are taught what to believe. We learn success is making money, having material possessions, a family, enjoying life. We learn to worry only about ourself, not to be concerned for others.

Those accepting this self-centered path through life, though they may achieve their goals, remain asleep, never understanding the genuine purpose of their life's journey. They live their life with their eyes closed, accepting the many struggles others endure as simply being a part of life.

Some though, may begin to open their eyes from their deep slumber, awakening to the possibility there may be more to life than success. They start to realize, as the first quiet messages from their spirit are sensed, everything they once believed to be true, may not be. The spirit accompanies every life; its purpose is to transcend ignorance and reach divine understanding, allowing us to help others realize this is their purpose in life as well.

When we follow our spirit's guidance, we open our eyes completely, fully awakening from our slumber. Selflessly sharing its wisdom and love with others will allow us to discover the genuine reason for our life's journey as well.

See Beyond Our Labels and Façade

With our birth, our labels begin. We are endlessly divided by race, sex, wealth, ethnicity, religion, and in hundreds of other ways. Though some labels may help organize society, they truly only serve to divide, rather than unite us. These divisions are the cause of prejudice, inequity, war, and many of humanity's self-imposed struggles and harmful emotions.

As we are growing up, many also develop a façade, an outer protective shell they use to disguise their true self. Though our façade does protect us, it also prevents others from getting to know our authentic self as well. We may have a family, many friends, but unless they can penetrate our defensive barrier, our interactions with others will be superficial.

It is only when we gaze beyond our labels and facade to the loving spirit within may we truly know another. Though we may all look, act, and believe differently, it has always been our similarities that truly define us, not our labels, façade, and differences.

Is There More to Life?

There may come a time in everyone's life, regardless of whether they believe in religion or have no belief at all, they may ask themselves this question: is there a reason we are alive? If we believe everything we were taught, we think we are alive to make money, allowing us to buy material possessions, have a family, and enjoy the best things life has to offer. Many in the world accept this self-centered view of life, resulting in immense inequity, insatiable greed by the wealthy and those in power, and the innumerable challenges and harmful actions many suffer resulting from living in a world dictated by these beliefs.

There are some who may awaken during their life though, sensing the first quiet messages from their spirit within. At this time, they may begin to question if there is another reason we are alive. As the messages from their spirit become clearer, they start to realize everything they learned and once believed to be true, was not. Wealth, material possessions, will not allow them to find meaning or purpose in their life, for these may not be found in a self-centered world.

With the embrace of the spiritual path, they now realize we are alive to selflessly share our wisdom and unconditional love, our spirit, with others, regardless of our differences, so everyone may succeed in life, not just ourselves. With this understanding we will discover the authentic answer to the question: why are we alive, as well.

How Many More?

How many more innocents must die? How many more must struggle through life, homeless, hungry, afraid? How many more people and other forms of life must we abuse before we wake up and understand none of this is right? We live in a self-centered world, immunized from the innumerable horrors and challenges of others, worried only about our own success and survival, with little concern for others.

We must each make a choice in our life. To continue to ignore the inequities and needless struggles resulting from living in such a world, or to view the world through a different lens, one where we treat everyone, regardless of our differences, with compassion and unconditional love.

By embracing the spiritual path, we would help everyone in need, understanding every person, regardless of our differences, is equally important and that we are alive to sincerely care and help each other, not to continue to ignore those who are needlessly struggling.

What is the Spirit and What is Spirituality?

The spirit is an ethereal presence joining a new life to provide it with guidance and meaning. It is a piece of god, our higher-self, inextricably connecting each life to another's. Only by joining our loving essence with the essence, the spirit within others, selflessly aiding each other in our time of need, will our lives have true meaning and purpose. Understanding this is the genuine reason for our life's journey, the lesson we are alive to learn.

The spirit is often in conflict with the ego, our self-centered beliefs. When the ego is dominant, which it is for most, there are abundant challenges, tragedies, and struggles, as our focus is only on what is best for ourselves, rather than others. When this happens, our spirit's messages are suppressed, overpowered by our dominant ego. This results in greed, prejudice, inequity, war, hunger, homelessness, and many of humanity's other self-inflicted challenges and harmful emotions.

We awaken when we sense the first quiet messages from our spirit within, letting us know we may be following the wrong path through life: the path of the ego. As our spirit's messages become clearer, we begin to realize everything we learned, accepted, and believed to be true, was not. It was a distraction meant to challenge our life choices, preventing us from understanding the genuine reason we are alive.

Spirituality is the belief we are alive to selflessly share our innate wisdom and unconditional love, our spirit, with others, in which a spirit is present as well. That each life, regardless of our differences, accomplishments, or genus, each with a piece of god within, is linked together, and only by helping each other, without motive or benefit, may we truly understand the genuine reason of our life's journey.

Unpacking Our Baggage in Life

Upon our birth, we begin filling our mind with baggage, often affecting our lives for many years. As we are socialized to accept society's norms, many of our beliefs, prejudices, and ideas about the world are formed. Living in a self-centered world, believing these things are true, result in much of the clutter we collect during our life. Though it does not take long to accumulate much of our baggage, often in the first five years of our life, it may take the rest of our life, if at all, to unpack it.

To unpack the baggage in our life we do not have to face every issue we have dealt with throughout our lives. Rather, we need to confront the underlying cause by challenging the self-centered beliefs we accept as true. We awaken when the first quiet messages from our spirit, present within every life, are sensed.

As we begin to realize everything we had learned, which is the cause of our clutter, was not true, our baggage begins to empty. With the complete acceptance of the spiritual path our bag is now totally unpacked, realizing, regardless of our differences, we are alive to selflessly share our spirit's wisdom and unconditional love to aid others in need. This is our true purpose in life.

The Paradox of Life

When we are first born the paradox of life begins. For with our first breath, the ego, our self-centered beliefs, is created. Our ego's only concern is what is best for us; it worries little about others. Its desire is for us to succeed in life by making enough money to allow us to enjoy the best things life offers.

We may first notice the paradox when, though we may have achieved our goals, have money, material possessions, a family, we begin to sense an uneasy feeling within, questioning if there may be more to life than just what we first believed. This feeling arises from our spirit, present within every life. Its messages of being equally concerned for everyone, rather than only ourselves, awakens us to question our learned beliefs.

Once we awaken, we may never go back to sleep. As we reevaluate our friendships, job, beliefs, we may make many changes in our life, now wanting to spend our lives selflessly helping others, rather than only being concerned for ourself. We soon begin to understand nothing we learned about living a successful meaningful life was true; that money, though necessary to survive, has little to do with success. Rather, genuine success in life may only be found with the complete embrace of the spiritual path, then selflessly sharing our spirit's inherent wisdom and unconditional love to help others become successful in their life as well.

The World in Which We Live

Humanity has a stark choice to make. They may choose to continue to live in a divided self-centered world of competition, prejudice, inequity, or they may spiritually evolve, choosing to live in a world of cooperation, acceptance, and unconditional love instead.

Simply look at the world today and throughout humanity's history to see what living in an egoistic world is like. Prejudice, greed, war, hunger, are but a few of the many problems resulting from the numerous divisions between us. There are some who are wealthy, have many possessions, and can enjoy life's pleasures. There are others though, who are homeless, hungry, struggling every day simply to survive. This is the world we live in, but it need not be.

With the spiritual evolution of humanity, every person would be treated equally; race, ethnicity, wealth, religion, would make no difference. No one would go hungry, be homeless, or struggle unnecessarily; everything would be uniformly shared with all. There would be no inequity, intolerance, avarice, as the equal importance of every life would be recognized. By accepting the loving spiritual path, selflessly helping everyone, regardless of our differences, every person may find true happiness, inner peace, eternal love, and discover genuine meaning and purpose in their life as well.

A Divided World

We live in a very divided world. We are taught from the moment of our birth to judge others by their race, ethnicity, religion, appearance, wealth, and in hundreds of other ways, each further separating us from each other. We are socialized to believe some people, because of their differences or accomplishments in the world, are better, their life more valuable than others. We even believe the lives of human beings, due to their intelligence, is more important than the lives of other forms of life. The result of living in such a world is prejudice, inequity, war, hunger, and numerous other needless struggles so many endure.

Though we look, believe, act differently, we live in one world, intimately linked by a spirit, a piece of god within, connecting every life to another's. Adopting the spiritual path, we realize there are no divisions or judgments. It matters not our differences, wealth, genus; every life is, and always has been, equally important, each having a symbiotic relationship not only with our planet, but with each other as well. It is only together, embracing our similarities rather than our differences, that our life's true purpose may be understood.

We Are All Children of the World

We grow up in a very divided world. We differentiate ourselves from each other by race, ethnicity, sex, religion, wealth, and in hundreds of other ways. Humanity has even created a caste system to further divide us. Those who are wealthy, famous, have prestigious jobs, are in the highest caste, while others who are poor, homeless, struggling, occupy the lowest caste. These divisions not only separate us, but also make some people believe they are better, their lives more important, than others. These self-centered beliefs are the cause of war, prejudice, inequity, and many of humanity's self-inflicted challenges throughout time.

In spirituality, there are no divisions, believing every life, regardless of our differences or accomplishments, is equally important. We are all children of god, whose spirit is within every life. No one person's life is, or ever has, been more important than another's. Only together may we flourish. Apart, embracing only our differences rather than our similarities, we are all destined to fail.

We Are Not Alone

We live in a self-centered world, often struggling alone to survive. The reality though, is we have never been alone. For within each of us is a spirit, a piece of god. Its purpose to allow us to explore deeper meanings in life. Our spirit, and the spirit within others, have always been there to help; we simply did not know how to ask.

Humanity's Hubris

Humanity's hubris is a belief mankind, since it is more intelligent and the dominant species on our planet, can do whatever it wants, regardless of the harm it may cause. This includes not only lower forms of life, but to each other, and our planet itself. There are those who even believe there are some people who are more deserving, better than others, due to any of the many differences there are between us. This hubris is the cause of endless wars, prejudice, inequity, and many other man-made problems and harmful emotions throughout humanity's brief existence on earth.

When we awaken, sensing the first quiet messages from our spirit within, we begin on a spiritual journey. We start to realize nothing we were taught about our importance in the world is true. It was a façade, an illusion, created by the ego, our learned beliefs, to serve its self-centered interests.

Every life, regardless of our differences or genus, and our planet itself, is infused with a spirit, a piece of god intimately linking each to the other. Only together, sharing our unconditional love and resources equally with all others, respecting the rights of our planet and every life on it, will humanity's hubris be mitigated and its spiritual evolution finally begin.

The Reason We Are Alive

Why are we alive? This question, asked for millennia, has only two possible, though quite contrary, answers. The first reason, believed by most, is to make money, buy material possessions, have a family, and do the best things life offers. This self-centered view of our purpose in life is the cause of prejudice, inequity, and the needless struggles and hardships of many seeking to survive in an indifferent world.

The other reason may be considered to be the antithesis of the first answer. Those who embrace this viewpoint believe we are alive to selflessly share our inherent wisdom and unconditional love, our spirit, to help others in need. One need not have money, material possessions, or anything else found in the world to accomplish this. They simply need a pure heart and be willing to selflessly share their essence, their spirit present within each, without motive or benefit, with all others.

Those who believe the former, when they approach death will discover nothing they accumulated in their life will accompany them. Though they may have led a successful life, when they die, their memory will rapidly fade; their life having been led without meaning. For those, however, who followed the spiritual path in life, though their body and ego, their learned beliefs, will perish when they die, their spirit will continue to live in perpetuity, within the spirit of all those they selflessly helped in their life. Their life will therefore be forever memorialized, having been lived with genuine purpose and meaning.

The Power of Spirituality

Most people believe power comes from wealth, fame, having a prestigious job, allowing us to have others do our bidding. Although these things may allow us to experience life more, this power is illusionary, for true power may not be found in a self-centered world.

Spirituality is the belief there is a piece of god, a spirit or soul, within every life, and because of this, each life is important, equal, and connected. A spirit guides us with its inherent wisdom and unconditional love on our journey through life. With the acceptance of the spiritual path comes genuine power. One need not have money, fame, or worldly possessions to uncover this power. It has always been there, hidden behind the acceptance of our self-centered views about life.

With enlightenment and the full embrace of the spiritual path, the genuine meaning of life becomes evident. The unleashed power of the spirit may allow miracles, such as those performed by Buddha, Mohammed, and Jesus, to occur. We each have the same abilities and power as these great prophets, though it will take a complete acceptance of the spiritual path for them to become apparent. By using this power to selflessly help others, the genuine purpose of our life's journey will have been realized.

The False Path

Before we are born we are enlightened. Within each life is a spirit, a piece of god accompanying each of us. The spirit is the source of divine wisdom and intuition. This is the path through life we are meant to follow. With our birth though, the ego, our learned beliefs, is created. Our ego has little concern for others, only being worried about our success and happiness in life.

As we learn how to survive in the world, our beliefs, prejudices, and fears are formed, often adopting these views for the rest of our life. Following the self-centered path of the ego leads us to chase a false path through life. War, hunger, homelessness; greed, inequity, prejudice, are but a few of the many problems experienced by chasing this illusionary path.

We awaken when we first sense the quiet messages from our spirit within, trying to remind us of our true purpose and path in life. Previously silenced by our dominant ego, we begin to realize everything we learned may not be true. As the messages of our spirit become clearer, we begin the arduous journey to rediscover what we once knew before we were first born and exposed to the false isolating beliefs of the world around us.

The Door

The door is a metaphor for why we go in and out of enlightenment. Every once in a while we may get a glimpse of what enlightenment feels like; an inner peace, overwhelming love, sensation of total understanding encompasses our entire being. But then something happens and this serene feeling we once felt is gone. We fall back into the daily patterns that have always dominated our life.

Picture a door on top of a hill. On one side of the door, living our life in a self-centered world, we are trying to survive, find happiness, love, and meaning in our life. Looking for these things in the world, believing they may be found by having money, material possessions, or being with another person, we struggle daily to find them. These things we so desperately search for though may not be found in the world. As long as we even partially believe they may be, though we may experience short periods of enlightenment after we climbed the hill and briefly passed through the door, we may never remain on the other side.

On the other side of the door is enlightenment. Within every life is a spirit, a piece of god present to give our lives meaning. Fully embracing the spiritual path through life, selflessly sharing the inherent wisdom and unconditional love of our spirit within, will bring enlightenment. To remain on the other side of the door, not be pulled back through it, accept the spiritual path, then selflessly help others do the same as well.

Spirituality and the First Five Years of Life

When a child is born their indoctrination into the world begins. With their first breath, the ego, which is everything we learn and believe to be true, is created. The first five years of a child's life are the most critical, as their beliefs, prejudices, and views of the world are formed. Often, if what they learned was detrimental to them, they may then spend the rest of their life asleep, trying to undo the damage done during their early formative years.

If a child is brought up with fear, worrying only about their own survival in the world, though they may be successful in life, become wealthy, famous, and do the best things life offers, they will not find meaning or purpose during their life's journey. For these things may never be found in a self-centered world. They must first be discovered within, where our spirit accompanies each of us through life.

It is possible though, to bring our children up with love rather than fear. Though they must be taught about the dangers in the world during the first five years of their life, they can be brought up in a loving environment, being taught the importance of selflessly sharing their unconditional love, their spirit, with all others. These children will understand the importance of every life, never judging others by their differences or accomplishments, realizing our true purpose in life is to love, not fear others. These children will be well-adjusted and therefore, be able to readily find happiness, inner peace, genuine love, and meaning during their life as well.

Sleep Well My Child

We live in a world of endless wars, random violence, prejudice, where survival may be measured in days, rather than years. We divide our world by race, religion, ethnicity, wealth, and in hundreds of other ways, believing the lives of some people are more important than others. These dangers result from living in a self-centered world, concerned only for what will benefit ourselves, rather than concern for others.

How may any child sleep well in such a world? They hear about others needlessly dying and struggling to survive every day. Because of this, rather than sleeping well, they have nightmares resulting in stress, anxiety, and fear.

We do not have to continue to live in such a world; we may choose to live in a world of love instead. It will take a monumental shift of consciousness, a spiritual evolution, though, for this to happen. To allow our children to sleep well, humanity must embrace the spiritual path through life, realizing there is a spirit, a piece of god present within every life intimately connecting each of us to the other and only together, selflessly helping each other without motive or benefit, may we all sleep well, allowing our children's nightmares to be changed to dreams of hope instead.

The Evolution of Humanity

Though the earth is billions of years old, humanity has only been present for a very short fragment of its existence. Their intelligence allowed them to evolve, eventually becoming the dominant species on our planet. About 11,000 years ago, the advent of formal religion first began. As religions slowly developed, the idea of god became an important part of human life.

Though religions began nobly, the original meaning of love, being selfless, helping others, and other altruistic beliefs began to take human definitions of what those words meant. When Jesus talked about loving all others equally, he meant selflessly, not conditionally depending on their beliefs, race, or ethnicity. Eventually, the pure spiritual beliefs religion first embraced deteriorated to the point they are barely recognizable now.

Humanity's evolution though is not yet complete. The next step in its evolution is spiritual, though quite different from the original spiritual beliefs of early religions. Spirituality believes there is a spirit, a piece of god present within every life, and therefore, each life, regardless of our differences or accomplishments, is equally important. Only together may humanity succeed, furthering its spiritual evolution and changing the direction of the world forever. Apart, as it has always been, they are destined to become a footnote in history.

Raising Our Frequency

Frequency is determined by which path in life we will follow. There are two main paths we each may pursue. One, the self-centered path of the ego, our learned beliefs. If we pursue this path, though we may be successful in life, our frequency will be quite low, as we will not recognize our true purpose in life.

The second path is the path of the spirit. The spirit is our higher-self, a piece of god accompanying each of us through our life's journey. Our frequency starts to increase when we awaken, sensing the first loving messages of our spirit present within each life. Our spirit guides us toward spiritual awakening and higher understanding. The more we selflessly share our spirit's wisdom and love with others, the higher our frequency climbs. When we give our spirit permission to become the primary guide in our life, our frequency will soar, as the genuine meaning of life will have been understood.

Our Spirit is Immortal

A spirit, a piece of god accompanies every life. The spirit is the guiding wisdom and truth within every life. The ego, our learned beliefs, is also present within each life; its ideas are often in direct conflict with our spirit. Whereas our ego is only concerned with what is best for us, our spirit is also concerned for the well-being of all others as well.

When we die, our body as well as our ego perishes. Those who have had a successful life, if it did not benefit others, their spirit will be readily forgotten, their life led without meaning or purpose. Our spirit, however, is immortal, returning to a higher vibrational level until it once again accompanies another life.

Our spirit though, by sharing its wisdom and love with others, also becomes part of every person we selflessly helped during our life. It therefore will become part of their spirit, passed down to all those that person influences as well. Although our body and ego do perish, our spirit will live within the spirit of others forever.

Living in a Spiritual World

We live in a self-centered world created by the ego, our learned beliefs, enforcing the idea we must always do what is best for ourselves, rather than to be concerned about others. It is the cause of prejudice, greed, inequity. It is also the source of war, hunger, and humanity's self-inflicted problems and harmful emotions.

Living in a spiritual world is quite different. The spirit, a piece of god present within every life. The spirit seeks knowledge, wisdom, and ultimate truth about existence. There are no divisions in such a world. Every life is considered equally important, regardless of race, ethnicity, religion, wealth, or any other differences. Each person is helped in their time of need and treated with unconditional love and respect for their life choices. Success in a spiritual world is only achieved when everyone succeeds together, understanding, alone, though we may have lived a prosperous life, it will have been without meaning or purpose.

Our Solitary Journey Through Life

Although we may have many friends, family, and other people we have met throughout our lives, it does not prevent us from being alone. All relationships and emotions, both positive and negative, including love, based on our self-centered beliefs are superficial, never allowing us to truly know or love another. When we interact with someone relying on these beliefs it is conditional, often hoping for a certain outcome to benefit ourselves. Though we may be surrounded by others, we are truly alone.

Within each life though, there is also an essence, a spirit, whose purpose is to share its inherent wisdom and unconditional love with the world. There are no alternative motives with the spirit; its messages are pure, untainted by life's journey. Therefore, when we communicate through our spirit, rather than the ego, our learned beliefs, directly to the spirit within another, our connection is genuine, allowing us to intimately unite our essence together.

To truly know another, see past their facade, talk to them from your heart, your spirit, directly to theirs. Only then will you not be alone and, in the process, discover the genuine meaning of life as well.

Our Footprint in Life

We each leave a footprint in life, defining if our life had meaning. Many believe wealth, fame, prestige will guarantee a large footprint. If that footprint though is not selflessly shared to benefit others, then this belief is an illusion, fostered by the self-centered ego, our learned beliefs. Though we may live a successful life, be wealthy, famous, accumulate many things, our footprint will be limited to just those we selflessly shared our success and love, our spirit, with. After we die, this is the only place our footprint will truly be remembered.

Those who leave the largest footprint in life selflessly share their spirit, their inherent wisdom and love unconditionally with all others. Wealth, fame, prestige, are not necessary to do so. Buddha, Mohammed, and Jesus are three great religious leaders who, though poor and unknow in many parts of the world, left an enormous footprint. Their spirit and beliefs continue to influence many in the world today. Their footprint persisted due to sharing their spirit, without motive or benefit, to improve the life of others.

Anyone, regardless of their circumstances in life, may leave a large footprint continuing its presence long after their demise. To do so, open your heart, sincerely share your unconditional love, your spirit, with others, aiding each to better their life's journey.

The Arc of Life

Life begins at conception. At that point, a spirit, a piece of god joins a new life. Our spirit's purpose is to transcend ignorance and reach divine understanding. If we allow it to do so, our life will have been lived with true purpose and meaning. Everything changes though when we are born. With our birth and exposure to the world, the ego, our learned beliefs, is created. Its only concern is us; it worries little about others.

Most people live their life believing everything they were taught. Most of humanity's problems and harmful emotions, including prejudice, greed, inequity, war, hunger, homelessness, are caused by following our self-centered beliefs in life. Though some may become successful, have wealth, fame, and be able to do the best things life offers, if they do not selflessly share their success with others, their life will have been lived without meaning or purpose.

We awaken when we begin to doubt the truth of all we learned. The first messages from our spirit begin to penetrate our egoistic barriers. Enlightenment is the complete acceptance of the loving spiritual path through life, realizing every life, regardless of our differences or accomplishments, each with a spirit within, is equally important and, only together, selflessly helping each other, may our life be truly meaningful.

The arc of life is complete when we die. Though our body and ego will both perish, if we fully embraced the spiritual path before our death, our immortal spirit will return to a higher vibrational plane, where it will remain joining other spirits. If we have not entirely accepted the spiritual lessons we are alive to learn though, our spirit will once again join another new life to try once more.

Nature versus Nurture

Are we nature, our innate spirit, genes, DNA? Or are we nurture, affected by what we learn in life, our ego? Both nature and nurture affect each of us and will remain with us throughout our entire life. We have a choice though which we will predominately allow to guide us through life.

Nurture is how we are affected by the world around us. Our beliefs, prejudices, ideas, and thoughts about success living in a self-centered world are all part of nurture. Living in a world dominated by nurture, our concern is only for what is best for ourselves, with little regard for others. It is a world of endless violence, hunger, homelessness; of greed, prejudice, inequity.

Nature, however, is more than just our DNA. It is also our spirit, the piece of god present within each of us. Our spirit's purpose is to seek knowledge, wisdom, and ultimate truth about existence. When we approach death, our body and ego will cease to exist. Our spirit, however, will continue to influence all we positively affected during our life.

The meaning of life is to selflessly share our spirit's wisdom and love, ignoring any differences between us, with all others, rather than continuing to blindly follow the false path of nurture we believe will bring us meaning in our life; it never could.

Living in the Shadows

Shadows are a combination of darkness and light. How dark our shadow is depends on where on the spectrum we are between the two. Darkness is fully accepting the beliefs of a self-centered world. Light is completely embracing the unconditional loving spiritual path through life. Most live on a continuum between the two, though lean toward the darker side of the spectrum, believing everything they were taught. This is the cause of most of humanity's self-inflicted problems, distrust, and harmful emotions.

When we awaken, beginning to question if everything we believe was true, we begin the arduous journey toward the light. As we start to understand it was not, our shadow lightens. With the acceptance of the spiritual path, our light brightens further. Though it will never return to its brilliance before we were born, the genuine purpose of our life, to rediscover our light within by selflessly sharing the inherent wisdom and unconditional love of our spirit with others, will now be realized.

Look at Your Reflection

Look in a mirror; what do you see? Is it the color of your skin, if you are male or female, how you are dressed, or any other unique features differentiating you from another? Most people believe they are what they see.

When we awaken, we begin to question if there is more to life than just our appearance and accomplishments. We begin to sense a spirit, within not only ourselves, but within all others as well. The spirit intimately links each of us to the other and is present to give our lives meaning. Now, when we gaze deeply at our reflection or into the eyes of another, we will start to be able to see past the façade and outer appearance, to the very essence present within every life.

With this understanding, we realize our body is but a shell, housing our mind, fragile ego, and spirit within. The spirit is a piece of god, a conduit for divine cosmic energy. Interacting on a spiritual level, the genuine meaning of our life's journey is recognized as our spirit now deeply connects with the spirit within others, in a union of genuine understanding, purpose, and eternal love.

Living a Happy Life

To many people a happy life means different things. For some who are quite poor, struggling in the world, being able to find a place to live, food to eat, clothes to wear, is enough to allow them to find some happiness on that day. For other people though, they look for happiness in the world, believing money, material possessions, a family, job, and other things will bring them what they seek. Though they may be successful and believe they are happy, happiness found in a self-centered world is fleeting, like the wind and rain after a passing storm. It often disappears due to stress and adverse circumstances in our life.

True happiness may only be found within, embracing the inherent wisdom and unconditional loving messages of our spirit, then it will only manifest itself when it is selflessly shared to benefit others. Doing so, we will also experience inner peace, know authentic love, and discover the genuine purpose of our life's journey as well.

The Path Back to Enlightenment

We are born enlightened, possessing the inherent wisdom and unconditional love of our spirit, a piece of god accompanying each of us through our life's journey. With our first breath, however, everything changes; the ego, our learned beliefs, is created. And with its dominant presence, most forget they were once enlightened. Instead, they whole-heartedly embrace the self-centered views of the world, concerned only for themselves, rather than others.

There may come a time in our life though, we awaken to the possibility everything we were taught may not be true. This happens when we begin to sense the first quiet messages from our spirit within, that had been previously silenced by our overpowering ego.

Enlightenment is the total acceptance of the spiritual path, and the realization everything we learned since we were born was a fabrication, an illusion, formulated by our ego, to challenge our choices in life. In an enlightened world, there would be no hunger, homelessness, war; no greed, inequity, prejudice, as the importance and parity of every life, regardless of our differences or accomplishments in the world, would be recognized. With this understanding, the spiritual evolution of humanity may finally begin.

Is Death the End?

We are born, we live our life, we die. Is that the end of life? Some religions believe, after death our spirit leaves our body, going either to heaven or hell, depending on if we were good or bad during our life. In spirituality, however, there is a third view of what happens after we die.

Spirituality believes there is a spirit, a piece of god present within every life, guiding us with its inherent wisdom and unconditional love meant to be shared with all others. Following the spiritual path through life will allow us to live a life of genuine meaning and purpose. With death, though our body and ego, our self-centered beliefs perish, our spirit does not; it is eternal. It returns to a higher plane of vibration, joining other spirits until it once again joins a new life. It also continues though, within the spirit of all those we selflessly helped during our life. Those who did not realize this and lived their lives concerned only for themselves, death may be the end. For those, however, who become enlightened, death is not the end of their journey. It is simply a transition to their existence's next challenges.

Human Rights

Humanity believes its rights supersede the rights of all other forms of life and our planet itself. There are those who even believe, due to their differences or accomplishments, their lives are more important than others. They view those who are poor, a certain race, religion, sex, or any of hundreds of other differences differentiating us from each other, as not as deserving of human rights as those who are wealthy, famous, a different race, or religion.

In spirituality, all human rights are the same; there is not one undeserving person in the world. It matters not our race, wealth, religion, beliefs, ethnicity, or any other differences there may be between us. Human rights mean every person has the right to have food, shelter, safety, and be helped in their time of need; that each has the same human right to life, liberty, dignity, love, and to live a life of genuine purpose and meaning.

Though we all look, believe, act differently, in truth, every person is exactly the same, each having a spirit, a piece of god within them, inextricably linking us to the other. Only by selflessly helping each other, equally sharing the resources on our planet, will all our lives have meaning, and our world begin to heal.

Living a Life of Meaning

Are we alive just to succeed in the world or is there another reason for our life's journey? If we accept the self-centered views of the world, we believe the reason we are alive is to make money, have material possessions, a family, and be able to do the best things life offers. When we follow this path through life, though we may be successful, if our success is not shared with others, our life will have been lived without meaning or purpose.

To truly live a life of meaning, we must come to the realization everything we thought would bring us success, happiness, love, and purpose in our life was not true. Money, possessions, or anything else found in a self-centered world will not allow us to find these. They must first be found within, where the spirit, our higher-self is present to help us discover and fulfill our life's purpose, then our success, happiness, love, and purpose must be selflessly shared with others to help them find these in their life as well. This is the genuine reason for our life's journey.

The Bus: A Journey Through Life

Before we are born, a spirit, a piece of god is present within every life. The spirit's purpose is to dissolve separation and experience oneness with all beings. With the total embrace of the spiritual path, our life will have been lived with genuine meaning and purpose and the lessons we are alive to realize will be understood.

Imagine a large, empty bus. With our first breath, we enter the bus. Waiting for us are our parents, brothers and sisters, grandparents, and perhaps a few other family members. Also, on the bus is our spirit, which accompanies each of us throughout our life. As the bus starts to move forward, our spirit begins to disappear as we begin to learn how to survive in a self-centered world. The ego's, our learned beliefs, only concern is us; it worries little about others.

As the bus keeps traveling forward, accepting and believing more of what we are taught, our spirit disappears even further. By the time we are adults, our spirit may be completely invisible, accepting everything we've learned in life is true. We therefore believe to live a successful life, we must make a lot of money, buy material possessions, and do the best things life offers. Our concern is focused solely on ourself, not others. Our spirit is now completely hidden, invisible, behind the barriers, the façade, the ego has built.

By this time, numerous people have gotten off the bus, as many of our relatives, friends, perhaps even our spouse, parents, or brothers and sisters begin to distance themselves from us. Now we are older; perhaps we have become successful in life, having money, material possessions, enjoying life's many pleasures. Though we have achieved our goals, when we look around our bus, it is empty. Though we may be wealthy, surrounded by many people, no one remains close to us, since we have not selflessly shared our success, love, or excess with any others.

Our spirit, however, has never left the bus. It remains invisible, hidden behind the acceptance of our learned beliefs. For some, there may come a time when they no longer wish to be alone on the bus. When this happens, they awaken, sensing the first messages of their spirit within, trying to remind them of their genuine purpose in life. With their awakening, their spirit begins to reappear in their life. At first, perhaps it is a shadow, though as its messages become clearer, they begin to realize everything they once believed to be true about success and meaning in their life, was not. The more they truly understand this, the more visible their spirit becomes.

The purpose of our life's journey is to completely fill our bus through our life by selflessly sharing our spirit's inherent wisdom and unconditional love, helping all others, regardless of our differences or if they are strangers, to live a successful, meaningful life as well.

Is One Life More Important Than Another's?

Is a Palestinian baby's life not as important as a Jewish baby? If someone is poor, homeless, unemployed, is their life not as important as someone who is wealthy, famous, has a prestigious job? These comparisons could include those of different races, religions, ethnicity, or any of hundreds of other differences between us.

In spirituality, there are no differences. Every life, regardless of appearance, beliefs, or life circumstances, is equally important, each having a spirit, a piece of god within, intimately connecting each of us to the other. It is only when we look past our superficial egoistic differences to the essence, the spirit within others, that will we truly understand the genuine purpose of our life's journey.

Tears in Heaven

With death, though our body and ego, our learned beliefs, will perish, our spirit accompanying each life, will continue its journey, returning to a higher level of vibration, joining other spirits in 'heaven'. God may be considered to be the entirety of all spirits linked together by their proximity, united as one, existing in an ether of universal wisdom and unconditional love.

The spirit is a piece of god. Its purpose is to dissolve separation and experience oneness with all beings. There are tears in heaven when humanity follows the self-centered path through life, rather than following the guidance of the spirit it was always meant to follow. This is the cause of many of humanity's self-inflicted challenges and harmful emotions.

The meaning of life is to recognize this, then selflessly share ours spirit's wisdom and love to help others understand this as well. With this realization, the genuine purpose for our life's journey will become evident.

The Wall

The wall is a metaphor; it surrounds our heart, trapping our spirit within. It is built by the ego, our learned beliefs, often when we are young to protect us from harm others may inflict on us with their words or deeds. The more we accept society's self-centered beliefs, the thicker our wall will be. The results of living in such a world are senseless violence, prejudice, inequity; a world where our dense wall is almost impenetrable.

The spirit is a piece of god present within every life. Its purpose is to encourage us to explore deeper meanings in life. For most, the messages of their spirit are hidden behind the thick wall their dominant ego built.

There may come a time in our life though, when we begin to question the truth of what we were taught. With this awakening, the first cracks in our wall appear, as our spirit begins to free itself from its confines. As the cracks broaden, the wisdom and loving messages of our spirit become clearer. With the complete shattering of our wall, allowing the benevolent loving messages and wisdom of our spirit to be selflessly shared to benefit others, we have learned the lesson we are alive to understand.

The Struggle

Struggle is part of every life. Though money may lessen its impact, no one may fully evade life's challenges. Even those who are successful and need not worry about food or shelter, still may struggle as they combat fears, depression, and anxiety, desperately seeking to find true love and happiness in their life.

Struggle, *despite* our circumstances in life though, need not continue. There are those who have very little food to eat or own many material possessions, whose challenges in life do not cause them distress. Once we realize the meaning of life is to follow the spiritual path, selflessly sharing our spirit's inherent wisdom and unconditional love with others, we no longer are concerned about life's daily challenges. Though we may live in a shanty, have few clothes or material possessions, have just enough food to eat, our struggle is nominal.

Money does make life easier, but it is not the underlying cause of all our struggles. It is only when we allow our spirit to be the primary guide in our life, may our struggles truly mitigate, and our life's meaning become apparent.

Open Your Heart

Opening your heart is extremely difficult to do, yet to awaken and begin the journey toward enlightenment, we must do so. When we are young, many create a façade to defend themselves. They avoid opening their heart, hiding behind the barrier they constructed to protect them from the pain that may occur if they lower their defenses. In a spiritual sense, opening our heart means letting down the egoistic barriers, the superficial front we have erected and display to the world, to protect ourselves from life's many challenges.

When we open our heart, we share our love, our spirit, selflessly, unconditionally, with all others, even if they do not respond in kind. Many who have awoken are afraid to fully remove their barrier. If they do not, though they may be awake, they will never become enlightened.

A Good Life

A good life may be different for each person. Some who are hungry, homeless, struggling every day, a good life may be to obtain enough food to eat, a place for shelter, clothes to protect them from the elements, simply trying to survive the day. For others, a good life is getting a well-paying job, allowing them to make enough money to buy material possessions, have a family, and enjoy life's many pleasures.

As we approach death though, the ego, our learned beliefs, realizes it will perish when its body does; it therefore releases its hold over our life at that time. Many may then begin to examine their life and what they believed a good life was. Realizing the money, possessions, experiences they had will not accompany them after their death, they begin to question if they truly had led a good life.

As they re-examine their life, without the presence of their controlling ego, they now begin to sense the messages from their spirit, a piece of god present within each of us; its messages had previously been silenced by their dominate ego. Our spirit's purpose is to help us discover and fulfill our life's purpose.

In spirituality, a good life may be experienced by anyone; it matters not their circumstances in life. Someone who is impoverished, homeless, hungry, barely surviving each day, but shares their essence, their spirit, selflessly with others, has had a good life, one far better than someone who may be wealthy, famous, have a prestigious job, who has not. For the person who is poor has understood the genuine purpose of life: following the guidance of their spirit, then selflessly sharing its wisdom and love to remind others to do the same as well.

The Loss of Innocence

We are born innocent knowing there is a spirit, a piece of god within each life, intimately connecting us to each other. The spirit is the transcendent aspect of human awareness that connects to something greater than the self.

With our very first breath though, everything changes as the ego, our learned beliefs, is created. And with the creation of the ego, our loss of innocence begins. The more we accept society's self-centered beliefs, the greater our loss of innocence becomes as the spirit's messages are silenced by our dominating ego.

The loss of innocence can be reversed, though will never totally go away. When we awaken, sensing the first quiet messages from our spirit within, we begin to question if everything we learned was true. As we realize little of it was, our loss of innocence starts to mitigate. The more we allow the spirit to guide our life, as it was always meant to, the more we will reclaim our innocence and understand the genuine purpose of our life's journey: to share our spirit's wisdom and love to help awaken others, so they too may discover their purpose in life as well.

Always Do the Right Thing

Every word we say and action we take should never hurt another. Anything harmful to anyone, whether it be verbal, physical, or in any other manner, is always wrong.

We are alive to share our spirit's wisdom and unconditional love, being sincerely concerned for others. Only together, always doing the right thing by selflessly helping and being considerate of each other without motive or benefit, may we each find true happiness, enduring love, and discover the genuine purpose for our life's journey as well.

The Human Condition

The human condition is the acceptance of everything we learn from the moment of our birth. We are taught, since humanity is superior and more intelligent than other forms of life, we need not concern ourselves about their existence. The human condition even teaches us there are some people, due to their wealth, fame, race, religion, or any of the many other differences between us, who are better, more deserving than others. This is the cause of prejudice, greed, inequity; of war, homelessness, hunger, and many of humanity's self-inflicted problems and harmful beliefs.

The human condition though is much more than this. If we go through life believing it is just everything we learned, then though we may be successful, we will die without fully understanding what the human condition truly is. If, however, we expand our definition of the human condition, accepting the importance of the spirit, a piece of god within us and every life, as an integral part of the human condition, then we will have truly understood not only what the human condition genuinely is, but the purpose of our life's journey as well.

Divisions in Life

We live in a self-centered world, endlessly divided. Race, ethnicity, religion, sex, wealth, are but a few of hundreds of ways we differentiate ourselves from each other. Our divisions are the cause of endless prejudice, inequity, violence, and many of humanity's self-inflicted challenges.

Though we may look, believe, and act differently, it is not our divisions that define us; rather, it is our similarities. We begin to understand this when we awaken, sensing the first quiet messages from our spirit within, questioning if everything we learned was true.

With the embrace of the loving spiritual path, instead of only seeing our differences, we now see beyond the superficial layers, the facade others present to the world, to the essence, the spirit within each. With this understanding we realize, regardless of our appearance, beliefs, accomplishments, or genus, we are inextricably linked together by the spirit and rather than being divided, we are united. By selflessly sharing our spirit's innate wisdom and unconditional love with others, our lives will have purpose and meaning.

Our Genuine Purpose

Why are we alive? We are taught to believe we are alive to succeed in life by making money, buying material possessions, having a family, enjoying the best things life has to offer. Those who only believe this self-centered view of life, though they may have achieved their goals, will have led a life lacking purpose.

To live a life of meaning, we must reunite with our spirit, a piece of god present within every life, selflessly embracing and sharing its inherent wisdom and unconditional loving messages with all others. With this awareness, the genuine purpose of life will become evident and the lessons we are born to learn will have been understood.

An Echo Within

With our birth the ego is created as we accept the self-centered customs and beliefs of the world. We learn success in life results from having money, material possessions, and being able to do the best things life offers. With this acceptance, our view of the world may become fixed, worrying only about our own happiness and success, rather than being concerned for any others.

There may come a time in our life though, we begin to hear a very faint echo within. This echo comes from our spirit, a piece of god that accompanies each life. With this awakening, we begin to question if there may be more to life than just what we had been told.

After we awaken, our life will never be the same again. We start to reevaluate everything we once believed to be true. The echo within is telling us we are alive to share our love and wisdom, our spirit, unconditionally with all others, and that every life, regardless of our differences or accomplishments in the world, is equally important.

Enlightenment is the total acceptance of the loving spiritual path and the sincere desire to selflessly help all others. By doing so, our life will have been meaningful and the reason for our journey, the purpose of life, will have been understood.

Choices in Life

There are but two choices in life: to follow the self-centered path of the ego, our learned beliefs, or the spiritual path, embracing the wisdom and unconditional loving beliefs of the spirit, a piece of god present within every life. By following the path of the ego, accepting everything we were taught is true, regardless of our success or accomplishments, we will never find true happiness, love, or meaning in our life. If, however, we embrace our spiritual center, allowing it to be the primary guide in our life, *despite* our circumstances in life, our life will be meaningful and worthwhile.

We each have a choice which path through life we will choose; we may alter our path at any time. Change must first come from within. Then when it is shared selflessly, unconditionally with others, we will find abundant happiness, enduring love, and genuine meaning in our life.

A World Without Boundaries

Humanity is divided by endless boundaries serving to isolate us from each other. Only by seeing past our differences to the essence present within each, may we mitigate these boundaries. When we do, instead of seeing only our differences, we will now begin to see our similarities instead.

In a spiritual world, boundaries do not exist, recognizing every life is equal, important, and connected. Understanding this, when we look at another what we now see is not their outward appearance, actions, beliefs, or façade, but rather their spirit, a piece of god present within each, knowing it connects each of us to the other.

Every life, regardless of our differences or accomplishments, has a spirit inextricably linking each of us to the other. When we see another realize we are all dependent on each other, and only together, living in a world without boundaries, may we each live a life of true purpose and meaning.

Forgiveness

The ego is our self-centered learned beliefs. Its desire is to foster our self-esteem and protect us from pain other people's words or actions may cause. To do so, it may encourage us to erect a barrier, a wall around our heart, isolating and distancing us from others. We then may carry this wound with us throughout the rest of our life.

We each have frailties; no one goes through life unscathed. If we wish to evolve spiritually and develop an understanding about our true purpose in life, we must completely forgive another for their human frailty, understanding it is caused by their ego trying to protect them. Only when we do, unconditionally forgiving them, regardless of the harm they caused or their faults, may we awaken to the genuine possibilities life truly offers.

Blaming Others

There are some people who go through life never accepting anything that happens to them as being their fault. Instead, they blame others or their life situation for all their hardships. When we do this, though we may become successful, we will never find true happiness, love, or meaning in our life.

Those, however, who embrace everything that happens, who do not blame others or the circumstances in their life for their challenges, accepting each as an opportunity to learn, will awaken, allowing them to begin on a path to discover the true purpose for their life's journey.

Areas of Grey

Areas of grey are things that happen in the world we know are wrong, yet we rationalize them as simply being a part of life. Humanity lives in such a world, justifying many things they see, read about, and hear. Innocents dying from war, starvation, random violence, their lives senselessly ended for no apparent reason. Prejudice, inequity, and other harmful human traits add to the many areas of grey resulting from living in a self-centered world.

In spirituality, there are no areas of grey; there is only light. For within every life is a spirit, a piece of god. Our spirit illuminates the world with a bright white light representing unconditional love. Selflessly sharing our love, excess, and helping all others is the message our light denotes. If we accept any areas of grey in our life, though we may have awoken, sensing the first messages from our spirit within, we will never fully travel the path to enlightenment.

Every life is equally valuable; wealth, prestige, race, or any other differences there may be between us, do not make one life more important than another's. Each, having a spirit, a blinding light within, intimately binds each of us to the other and to the universe itself. Only together, aiding each other without motive or benefit, will our lives truly have purpose and be meaningful.

A Spiritual Evolution

Humanity, being the dominant species on our planet, believe since they are superior to all other forms of life they have the right to decide for all. There are even some people who believe their life, due to their wealth, race, religion, or any other comparison, is more important than another's. Living in such a self-centered world, concerned only for ourselves, there is greed, prejudice, inequity; war, starvation, intolerance.

There will come a time though when humanity will evolve; this evolution will be spiritual. When this happens they will realize, regardless of our differences, accomplishments, or genus, each life, with a spirit, a piece of god within, is equally important. With this realization, the senseless struggles and needless deaths caused by humanity's indifference and arrogance will begin to be mitigated, as they finally understand they must equally respect each other, all other forms of life, and our planet itself, if we are all to survive and live a life of genuine purpose and meaning.

Between Life and Death

Did we live a meaningful life? After we are born we are taught to be successful we must get a good education, make money, own material possessions, have a family, and do the best things life has to offer. The reason we are alive though, has little to do with money, prestige, possessions, or anything else found in the self-centered world.

To live a meaningful life, we must remember there is a spirit, a piece of god present within not only each of us, but all others as well. Selflessly sharing our spirit's inherent wisdom and unconditional love with all, regardless of our differences, is the reason we are born, the lesson we are here to learn. By realizing this between our birth and death, we will have led a meaningful life, understanding the genuine purpose of our life's journey.

Everything We Learn in Life is an Illusion

We live in a world where we are taught to believe some people are more important than others. Due to their wealth, fame, job, their race, ethnicity, religion, they think some lives are more valuable than other's.

Everything we learn in life though, is an illusion, created by the ego, our self-centered beliefs, serving to isolate rather than unite us. We awaken when we first begin to sense our spirit within, questioning if what we learned was true. We become enlightened when we realize none of it was.

The Untouchables

We live in a world where we are divided into castes. There are those we consider worthwhile and others we consider untouchables, at the very bottom rung of society. Those in the top caste often are wealthy, famous, have a very prestigious job, believing their lives are more valuable than the lives of all those in castes below them.

The untouchables, in the lowest caste, may include those of a certain race, ethnicity, sex, or the homeless, poor, uneducated, struggling to survive every day. When those in higher castes pass by them, they often divert their eyes not wanting to acknowledge the untouchables exist, believing they are a stain on humanity. This is the world we live in, a world of the ego, our learned beliefs, accepting certain people are more deserving than others.

In spirituality, there are no castes, no untouchables. Every person, regardless of wealth, race, ethnicity, or any other comparison we may make, is equally important. The life of a poor, homeless, struggling person is every bit as valuable as someone who is wealthy, famous, or the president of a country. We are all connected, intimately linked by a piece of god, a spirit present within each of us. Only together, selflessly helping each other, recognizing the equal importance of every life, will we all find genuine meaning and purpose in our life. Apart, we will find neither.

Enduring Inner Peace

Many believe they will find inner peace if they achieve their life goals by making money, having material possessions, a family, and doing the best things in life. Yet most who have all these things still are unable to experience lasting inner peace.

True inner peace may never be found in a self-centered world. It may only come from within, where a spirit, a piece of god accompanies each of us in our journey through life. Though we may achieve our goals, without understanding the genuine reason for our life's journey, to selflessly share our spirit's wisdom and unconditional love with others, inner peace will be fleeting, often vanishing with the uncertainties and stresses of life.

With the complete embrace of the spiritual path, enduring inner peace will surround our entire being, and our spirit will forever become a part of everyone we share our inner peace and unconditional love with in our life.

Helping Each Other

We live in a competitive world. Our self-centered view of life is the cause of many of humanity's self-inflicted challenges and harmful emotions. War, hunger, homelessness; prejudice, greed, intolerance, are but a few of the numerous problems resulting from living in such a world.

When we begin on a spiritual path, sensing the first messages from our spirit within, we awaken to the possibility there may be more to life than just what we learned. Even if we become successful, wealthy, famous, have many material possessions, alone, not helping others, we will have lived our life without meaning.

True success in life has little to do with our accomplishments in the world. One need not have wealth, fame, or possessions to be successful. Genuine success may only be achieved when we selflessly share our success to help all others succeed in their life as well.

Heaven and Hell

Religion introduced humanity to the idea of heaven and hell, teaching heaven is above us, joyous, peaceful, full of love, somewhere in the universe, and hell below us, full of fire and brimstone. In spirituality, heaven and hell are on earth.

Hell begins when we are born with the acceptance of the self-centered beliefs of the world. By blindly believing everything we are taught, assuming it will allow us to find happiness, love, and meaning in our lives, we live in hell. This belief results in a world where there is war, greed, prejudice, inequity, and many other harmful actions and emotions humanity inflicts on each other.

Heaven is discovered once we fully accept and embrace the loving spiritual path within. With this understanding, we selflessly share our spirit's innate wisdom and unconditional love with others, helping them awaken and begin a quest to find heaven on earth as well.

Every Injustice Must Be Challenged

How long can we watch children and innocents needlessly die from random violence, hunger, indifference? How long may we ignore the countless struggles and hardships so many endure?

In spirituality, every life, regardless of our differences, is equally important. For humanity to awaken, they must no longer ignore when harm is done to another. It matters not if the injury is verbal, physical, or from war, prejudice, starvation, or in any other manner.

Apart, continuing to accept the self-centered status quo, nothing will change. Only together, realizing the genuine value of every life, each connected to the other by a spirit, a piece of god within, may we truly change the world.

Every injustice causing harm to another must be challenged. We may no longer pretend we are ignorant of other's pain and struggles; instead, we must protect each other and selflessly help each in their time of need.

See the World Through a Different Lens

How many more must needlessly suffer before we start to sincerely care about each other? Their struggles result from living in a self-centered world, concerned only about what is best for themselves, while ignoring the hardships of others.

Perhaps it is time to view life through a different lens; one where we treat all others, regardless of our differences, with compassion and love, rather than indifference and fear. Only then may humanity finally start to evolve, and the many self-inflicted problems caused by living in such a world begin to be mitigated.

To Truly Know Another

Living in a self-centered world, reading books, watching movies, observing others, we learn how we are supposed to act, think, and treat others. Though we may believe we understand how others feel, we do not. Our beliefs are simply a reflection of what we learned.

To truly know another, look beyond their appearance and façade. If you gaze at them intently, in between your random thoughts, you will sense their spirit within, allowing you to forge an intimate loving bond, as your souls merge together as one.

Our Only Genuine Emotion

All emotions resulting from our experiences in life are not genuine. Even those we consider positive, if they are conditional, shared with the expectation we will receive something in return, they are superficial.

The only genuine emotion, love, comes from within, where our spirit, a piece of god accompanies every life. This type of love is shared unconditionally, selflessly, with all others, always given without motive or benefit.

Open your heart, selflessly share your essence, your spirit with others. Only then, may you really know what love is and, in doing so, discover life's true purpose as well.

Living a Good Life

Many people believe living a good life means making enough money to have a house, family, material possessions, and be able to do the best things life offers. This self-centered belief, focused only on what is best for ourselves, is the cause of most of humanity's self-inflicted problems and harmful emotions.

With the embrace of spirituality, there is a realization a good life has little to do with money or our accomplishments in the world. That someone who is poor, homeless, struggling, may live a far better life than another who is successful.

Understanding there is a spirit, a piece of god present within every life, a good life will be lived when we selflessly share our spirit's innate wisdom and unconditional love with others. Anything else is simply an illusion, fostered by the ego, our learned beliefs, to challenge our life choices.

Live Your Life With Love

To evolve spiritually, never do, say, or harm another in any way. The only emotion we should ever share is unconditional love, selflessly given without motive, to benefit all. It is only when we truly recognize this, may we awaken and begin the journey to understand our true purpose in life.

Ego, Spirit, Awakening, & Enlightenment

When we begin our spiritual journey, we hear about the ego, spirit, awakening, and enlightenment, but it is difficult to truly understand what they are. This is a simplified explanation as to what each is.

The ego is everything we learn and accept is true in our life from the moment we are born; it represents our human-self. The ego's only concern is what is best for us; it worries little about others. It wishes to build our self-esteem, often by proving our superiority to others. It is also the cause of many of humanity's self-inflicted challenges in the world.

The spirit is a piece of god, present within every life, not only human, but within all other forms of life as well. It is an ethereal entity, accompanying every life to share its inherent wisdom and unconditional love to help guide our life's choices. The spirit's messages are often muted by our dominate ego; its messages, therefore, mostly go unnoticed. If we only follow the path of the ego, never sensing our spirit's messages, though we may have lived a successful life, having achieved all our goals, our life will have been led without meaning or purpose.

Awakening begins when we first detect our spirit's quiet messages sneaking past our ego's defenses, making us start to question our self-centered beliefs in life.

Enlightenment is the complete acceptance of the spiritual path through life. It is the realization, only by selflessly sharing our spirit's wisdom and unconditional love with all others, will our life have been lived with genuine purpose and meaning.

Spirituality and the Law

There are some laws necessary to protect people against others who may cause them grievous harm, but there are many other laws that are unjust, immoral, and must be challenged. Laws, such as those discriminating against others due to their race, religion, sex, are but three of many laws ethically wrong and must be universally condemned. Laws are created by humanity and often are influenced by the prejudices and beliefs of those in power, rather than by those who only want what is best for all.

Any law causing harm to another in any way is wrong and must be contested. To know if a law is improper, simply ask yourself how you would feel if it were applied to you or someone you love. Only by always doing what is right not only for us, but each other as well, regardless of our differences, may we further the spiritual evolution of our planet, allowing our children to grow up in a world of genuine love and equality, rather than to continue to live in an immoral world of prejudice and injustice.

Inhumanity

After we are born, we are taught how to survive in a self-centered world. We learn to be concerned only about ourselves and our success in the world, rather than to worry about others. This egoistic view of the world is the underlying cause of inhumanity. It is the reason for war, hunger, homelessness; for prejudice, greed, inequity, and many of mankind's other harmful beliefs and actions.

Humanity is sincerely caring about others by sharing our inherent wisdom and unconditional love, our spirit, to help all in need. Living in a humane world, there would be no hunger, homelessness, prejudice. These man-made problems would fade away along with most others, as the resources on our planet would be equally shared. We would understand every life, regardless of our differences, accomplishments, or genus, is equally important, inextricably linked to each other by a spirit within, and only together, selflessly helping each other, may we all live in a humane world and discover genuine meaning and purpose in our life as well.

In Another Life

We live in a self-centered world, taught from our first breath there are some people who, due to our differences, are better, more deserving than others. To understand what such a world is like, simply open your eyes and see. It is a world of inequity, greed, prejudice; of war, hunger, needless struggle. These are but a few of the numerous problems resulting from living in such a world.

In another life, picture a world that has spiritually evolved. In that world, we would realize there is a spirit, a piece of god present within every life, and only by selflessly sharing our spirit's unconditional love, knowledge, and wisdom about existence with others, will we all survive and reach our full potential. Instead of only worrying about ourselves, concern would be for everyone, all life on our planet, and for the earth itself. We would understand no one life is, or ever has been, more important than another's. It matters not religion, race, wealth, genus, or any of the other divisions between us. We are all connected, intimately linked by a universal spirit, and only together, selflessly helping each other, will humanity spiritually evolve, and this other life become a reality.

Heartlessness

We live in a heartless world where we tolerate the unthinkable. We accept some people are needlessly struggling, starving, homeless, while others live in luxury. We tolerate inequity, bigotry, avarice. We accept the reality of unending wars and the needless deaths of innocents due to humanity's greed, prejudice, and self-centered concern for itself. We treat our planet and all who inhabit it with disrespect, believing humanity is more deserving and need not concern itself with harming others or the planet that sustains us all. We believe money and material possessions define success. None of these things are or ever were acceptable.

We may choose though, not to live in such a world. Instead, we may treat others humanely, by selflessly sharing our unconditional love and excess to help all in need. We are alive, the meaning of life, is to help each other, without motive or benefit, so everyone, regardless of our differences, may reap the benefits of life. This is the lesson we are alive to learn.

Living in an Egoistic World

We live in a self-centered world where we are taught what to believe and what success is. We learn to be concerned only about what is best for ourselves, rather than to worry about others. We therefore believe to succeed in life we must make enough money to buy material possessions, have a family, and be able to do the best things life offers. Living is such a world, there is greed, prejudice, inequity; hunger, homelessness, senseless violence, and many other man-made problems and harmful emotions experienced throughout the world.

Little we were taught though is true or will allow us to be successful and live a meaningful life. To live such a life, we must first look within, where our spirit exists, inextricably connecting each of us to the other. Only then, when we selflessly share our spirit's wisdom and unconditional love with others, may we truly life a meaningful successful life and discover our life's genuine purpose as well.

Are We Better?

Are we better than another because of our race, ethnicity, religion; our sex, wealth, job, or any of hundreds of other comparisons we may make? Is the president of a country better than the janitor who empties their trash? Are human beings better than animals or any other form of life?

If you believe the answers to these questions are yes, you remain asleep, accepting the erroneous self-centered beliefs of humanity. If, however, you realize every life, regardless of its differences, accomplishments, or genus, is equally important, each having a spirit, a piece of god within, inextricably linking us to each other and to the universe itself, you have awoken, beginning a spiritual adventure to discover life's true meaning.

Living a Successful Life

We are taught success in life means having a good job, making money, buying material possessions, having a family, and doing the best things life has to offer. We believe when death approaches, if we have done all these things, we have led a successful life.

For some, though they may have achieved all their goals, they begin to sense there may be more to life than just what they were told and believed to be true. This awakening comes from their spirit within, as its first messages begin to be detected.

In spirituality, nothing listed above will guarantee success. One need not have money, material possessions, or anything else found in the world to have led a successful life. A poor, homeless person with few possessions may do so. Genuine success may only happen when we embrace the spiritual path, selflessly sharing our inherent wisdom and unconditional love, our spirit, with all others, allowing them to be able to lead a successful life as well.

Look Into My Eyes

We are each different in many ways. It is the belief our differences make some lives more valuable than others though, that are the cause of war, inequity, prejudice, and many of humanity's other self-inflicted problems and harmful beliefs.

When we awaken, beginning to question if everything we were taught is true, we start to notice our similarities instead, rather than only our differences. We begin to gaze past the superficial appearance and beliefs of another.

If we look intently enough, we will see, behind our outward appearance, beliefs, and the facade we have learned to present to the world, is a spirit, a piece of god, intimately connecting us to each other.

Look deeply into the eyes of another. If you do, you may be able to sense their spirit, present within their life as well. It is then we will truly understand we are not different at all; rather we are linked in a common journey through life, and only together, despite our differences, will we each discover our true purpose in life.

Living in Peace

What is peace? Is it the lack of war? This type of peace is fleeting, temporary, lasting only until the next dispute. Living in a self-centered world of greed, prejudice, inequity, it is only a matter of time before the desires of those in power challenge others, erupting once again in conflict.

There is, however, a more lasting peace. This peace comes from within, originating from the inherent wisdom and unconditional loving messages of our spirit, accompanying every life. These messages are about selflessly helping each other, never judging anyone no matter our differences, and sharing our excess and spirit's wisdom and love with all others. Following the spiritual path through life will bring an extraordinary enduring inner peace, as the realization of the lessons we are here to learn will have been understood.

Love

When we are born we know only unconditional love. At the moment of our birth though, the ego, our self-centered beliefs is created, as we start to learn what love is by watching movies, reading books, observing the world. This type of love though is conditional, fleeting, until conflict or changes in our life, may alter our deep feelings for another.

There is another form of love, however, that is genuine, long-lasting, and meaningful. It is inherent, present within each life, emanating from our spirit, a piece of god accompanying every life. It is given selflessly, without motive or benefit, to sincerely share our love and light with another.

Many, embracing the former, think they know what love is; they do not. Therefore, they never truly experience pure love during their life. When we embrace the latter form of love though, not only will we experience what love truly is, but we will also discover the genuine reason for our life's journey as well.

Looking for Meaning

Many believe meaning in our life may be found through having money, material possessions, a good job, family, or any of the many other things we were taught would make our life worthwhile. Meaning though, found in a self-centered world is often fleeting, until circumstances or changes in our life end our feelings of worth.

To find genuine meaning in life, we must first discover it within, where the spirit, a piece of god is present to help us explore deeper meanings in life. Any other belief, though we may believe it gives our lives meaning, does not. It is an illusion, created by the ego, our learned beliefs, to detour our spiritual journey.

We awaken when we start to sense the first quiet messages from our spirit within, reflecting doubt whether meaning may truly be found in the world. As the messages become clearer, we begin the arduous journey to find the genuine reason we were born: 'to fully embrace the spiritual path by unconditionally sharing our spirit's wisdom and love with all others, so they too may discover genuine meaning in their lives as well'.

Look Past Our Differences

We live in a world of differentiation, labeling ourselves to accentuate our differences from others. We are rich, poor, male, female, Buddhist, Muslim, or any of hundreds of other comparisons emphasizing our contrasts. These differences are the cause of endless wars, prejudice, inequity, and many of humanity's self-inflicted problems and harmful emotions. They occur as some wish to prove their superiority to others because they may look, act, or believe differently than they do.

To bring genuine change to the world though, we must look beyond our differences to our similarities instead, challenging our self-centered views of the world. Every life, each with a spirit, a piece of god present within, intimately links each of us to the other. Only by selflessly sharing our spirit's unconditional love and inherent wisdom with each other, may we not only change the world, but discover our true life's purpose as well.

One Life

Is one life more important than another's? Is someone's life, because of their race, ethnicity, religion, wealth, or any of hundreds of other comparisons we may make, more valuable than someone who is different from them? Is the life of a wealthy, famous president of a country more valuable than a poor, homeless child's life? Is a human life more valuable than an animal's? Many would answer yes to the above questions, believing it is our differences, rather than our similarities, that define us.

We awaken when we start to question this premise, sensing the first messages from our loving spirit within. We begin to realize, regardless of our accomplishments, appearance, beliefs, or any other differences between us, one life is, and never has been, better than another's. Every life, each with a spirit, a piece of god within, is equally valuable. With enlightenment, we finally understand the answers to each of the above questions is no.

Never Hurt Another

We live in a self-centered world believing we must worry only about ourselves, rather than being concerned for others. Therefore, if it benefits us, we feel we may harm others with our words, actions, or deeds. The ego, our learned beliefs, encourages us to do this to show our superiority to another.

Any harm though, to anyone must never be accepted. It not only injures the person it is directed at, but those who cause the harm as well, further distancing each from their spirit within. We are alive to help not hurt, be compassionate not uncaring, love not hate, each other. Only when we treat each other as we each wish to be treated ourselves, may our life's genuine purpose and meaning finally be understood.

My Spirit Weeps

My spirit weeps when it looks at the world seeing the needless deaths of children, innocents, and others, dying from random violence, starvation, and other man-made avoidable tragedies. It weeps because humanity has the ability now to end these unconscionable sorrows. Technology exists today to grow enough food to feed the hungry, build enough homes to shelter the homeless, end climate change. There simply is not the will to do so.

Every life is inextricably connected to each other by a piece of god, a spirit within each. The spirit's purpose is to transcend ignorance and reach divine understanding. When we follow our spirit's direction, the purpose of our life, the lessons we are alive to learn, will be understood.

To stop my tears humanity must hear my message and understand the equal importance of every life, regardless of their differences. They may begin to do so by equally sharing their resources and unconditional love with all, so each may thrive. Only then may my sorrow end, and the genuine meaning of humanity's journey be understood.

Seeing the World with Love

We each have a choice how we see the world. If we view the world through a fearful lens, we will see a world of greed, prejudice, inequity; a self-centered world focused only on our own survival, with little concern for others. If, however, we see the world through a lens of love, though we understand our basic needs for survival must be met, we realize everything else is truly not important. Rather than being concerned only about our own success in the world, our focus now shifts to helping others succeed as well.

Living in a world of love, there is no hate, judgement, inequity. There are no castes, endlessly dividing humanity by sex, religion, ethnicity, wealth, race, or any of hundreds of other ways we differentiate ourselves from each other. Every person, each having a spirit, a piece of god within inextricably linking us to the other, would be treated equally, selflessly aided in their time of need. By sharing our spirit's inherent wisdom and unconditional love with others, we may help awaken their spirit within, allowing us all to live in a world of love, instead of continuing to live in a world of endless fear.

Our Barriers

Some learn to protect themselves by creating a barrier, a façade, preventing pain that may result from the words, actions, or deeds of others trying to harm them. Though this protection allows them to survive in the world, it also prevents them from truly knowing their authentic-self, their spirit within, as well.

Only by lowering our shield may we know how life is genuinely meant to be lived. Doing so will also allow us to begin a journey to discover our life's genuine purpose as well.

Struggles in Life

Struggles in life are part of the journey. For some, the struggle is trying to survive every day, seeking food, shelter, constantly worried about safety. For others, who need not be concerned about these things, their struggles may be emotional, dealing with stress, anxiety, depression, as they seek to find love and happiness in a self-centered world.

We need not struggle alone though. Within each of us is a spirit, a piece of god always there to aid us in our times of need. To mitigate our challenges, we simply need to ask, then quietly listen to the soft loving messages in between our thoughts, from our spirit within.

It is how we react to our struggles though, that will determine our future. For many, rather than learning and benefiting from their trials, they blame others or circumstances in their life for their problems. Struggles though, are a lesson, meant to encourage us to reevaluate our life's choices. If we embrace our struggles, rather than find fault from them, they may help awaken us to the false illusionary lessons we learned, believed, and accepted as true, beginning us on a path to discover our true purpose in our life.

The Cult of Humanity

The cult of humanity began when human beings became the dominant species on the planet. They believe, due to their intelligence, they have the right to do anything they wish, regardless of the effects it may have on other forms of life, our planet, or even on each other. Due to their many differences, humanity further separates themselves into castes, divided by race, ethnicity, religion, wealth, or any of hundreds of other ways they differentiate themselves from each other.

Some therefore believe the lives of some people are more valuable than others, justifying their prejudices and lack of concern for those different from them. The result of the cult of humanity are endless wars, hunger, inequity, prejudice, and an almost endless list of mankind's self-inflicted problems and harmful emotions.

To mitigate this cult, the human race must awaken, realizing they are not, and never have been, better than any other form of life or each other. Only by truly understanding every life, regardless of our differences, accomplishments, or genus, is equally important, each having a spirit, a piece of god within, then sharing their spirit's wisdom and unconditional love selflessly to help all others, may the cult of humanity end and their spiritual evolution finally begin.

The Circle of Life

Life begins before birth, when a spirit, a piece of god joins a new life. The spirit knows only one emotion, unconditional love meant to be shared selflessly with all others. There are no distractions, no concept of me or I; the spirit knows only us.

With birth, however, the ego, our learned beliefs, is created. Its only concern is me or I, worrying only about what is best for you; it has little interest in others. As we are socialized into the world, our values, prejudices, and ideas about success are formed. We therefore adopt many of humanity's self-centered beliefs, believing success in life is making money, buying material possessions, having a family, and enjoying the best things life offers.

An interesting thing happens as we approach death. At that point, the ego, since it will perish when its body does, loses interest in trying to influence us. The messages of our spirit, therefore, silenced throughout our life by our ego's dominance, may finally be heard. We now realize nothing we had once believed about success was true. Though we may have had wealth, fame, material possessions, a family, our life was lived without purpose or meaning. We now understand to have led a genuinely successful meaningful life, we needed to selflessly share our success with others, allowing them to find success in their life as well.

With death, the spirit will then return to a higher vibrational plane, until it once again joins another new life, restarting the circle of life once more.

The Gift of Life

Life is an extraordinary gift. Most, believing everything they have learned, define success as making money, having material possessions, a family, and doing the best things life offers. They live their entire life believing and accepting these self-centered ideas. Though they may have been successful and achieved all their goals, they squandered their gift of life, not understanding their true purpose or taking advantage of the opportunities life has given them.

Our body is simply a shell, in which a spirit, a piece of god accompanies us. The gift of life, the reason we are born is to transcend ignorance and reach divine understanding. We awaken when we sense the first messages from our spirit within, wondering if there may be more to life than what we were told.

The gift of life may only be truly understood though, when we realize everything we once believed to be true was not. It was an illusion, created by the ego, our learned beliefs, to challenge our choices in life. Only by fully embracing the spiritual path through life may we truly appreciate the gift of life we have been given and learn the lessons we were born to understand.

The Future of Humanity

There are but two options for humanity's future: extinction or evolution. Continuing along the current unsustainable path, where prejudice, war, inequity, are accepted as a normal part of life, the only possible outcome is extinction. Climate change, nuclear war, drought, disease, will eventually end humanity's brief era on our planet; they will simply become a footnote in history.

There is another option, though time for change is rapidly fading; it is a spiritual evolution. No longer may we sit idly hoping for change, accepting everything that is happening is inevitable; it is not. Most of humanity's self-inflicted problems and harmful emotions result from living in a self-centered world, where concern for the individual takes precedence over concern for others. We have the technology and ability now to end hunger, climate change, nuclear proliferation, and many of the other challenges in the world today. To do so though, humanity must evolve by accepting the wisdom and unconditional loving messages of their spirit within, then selflessly share those messages to improve the lives of all others.

The Flag of Humanity

We live in a world of endless division, separating ourselves from each other by race, ethnicity, wealth, and in hundreds of other ways. It is these divisions that lead to many of humanity's self-inflicted problems in the world. Rather than living under one flag, we live under many, identifying with the flag of our country, religion, sex, or any of the many other isolating flags we choose to live under.

Though we may look, act, believe differently, in truth, we all live under one flag, united by a spirit, a piece of god present within each of us, inextricably linking us to each other. By embracing the loving spiritual path, acknowledging our commonalties rather than our differences, we will understand we truly are one people, not many, living under one flag, made up of a rainbow of colors, beliefs, and differences. Only by recognizing our similarities and intimate connection to each other, will the hate, prejudices, and wars end, allowing us all to live in a world of love, acceptance, and peace instead.

The Eyes We See the World Through

We live in a self-centered world worrying only about ourselves, rather than others. It is a world of greed, prejudice, inequity. If we see the world only through these eyes, we will live in a world of fear. Many of humanity's self-inflicted problems and harmful negative emotions result from living in such a world.

We need not continue to live in fear though. Rather, we may choose to see the world through a lens of love instead, by selflessly sharing our spirit's unconditional love with others. In this world we would share our excess so everyone may be fed, housed, loved. Race, religion, ethnicity, wealth, would no longer divide us. Instead, we would all be united by our spirit within, connecting each of us to the other, helping all in need. Seeing the world through a lens of love, we will experience an extraordinary feeling of inner peace, as the genuine purpose of our life's journey becomes evident.

Stress

Stress is a part of life. Regardless of our circumstances, no one may escape it. Though some worry daily, seeking shelter, sustenance, safety, even those who have found success may stress about other things. The underlying cause of most stress though is living in a self-centered world, where concern for the individual is more important than concern for others.

There is a way to alleviate stress, though it will take a shift of consciousness to realize it. Within every life is a spirit, a piece of god present to give our lives direction and meaning. The spirit's purpose is to dissolve separation and experience oneness with all beings.

When we allow our spirit to become the primary guide in our life, our stress, caused by living in a self-centered world, begins to dissipate, replaced by knowing we may always be helped in our time of need by our spirit and the loving spirit within all others as well.

The Great Illusion

The great illusion begins with our first breath, when the ego, our learned beliefs, is created. We are taught success in life is making money, buying material possessions, having a family, and being able to enjoy life's many benefits. We adopt our prejudices and views of the world as we are socialized to accept society's beliefs. The result is we live in a self-centered world, isolating ourselves from each other. Believing there is little we may do to bring genuine change, we accept the many senseless deaths from war, random violence, starvation, as part of life. We withdraw ourselves into a cocoon, imagining these things do not happen. As long as humanity accepts the great illusion, nothing will change.

When we awaken, sensing the first quiet messages from our spirit within, we begin to reexamine society's rules, questioning if they are truly necessary. We now begin to wonder if we may bring change to the world by helping others, ending their unnecessary struggles.

As the loving messages of our spirit become clearer, we begin to challenge the great illusion, discovering much of what we were taught was a deception and is the cause of many of humanity's self-inflicted problems and harmful emotions. With the complete acceptance of the spiritual path, realizing the equal importance of every life, the great illusion is mitigated, leaving in its wake a world of love and compassion, rather than a world of hate and indifference.

The Soul

Humanity believes, due to its dominance and intelligence, their lives are more important than animals, trees, or any other form of life. They therefore needlessly exploit lower life forms when alternative choices are now available. Within every life though, is a soul, a spirit, a piece of god, connecting each life to another's. Look deeply into the eyes of any animal. Can you not see a sentient being within? Is the soul of an animal not as important as a human soul? Is the soul of one person more important than the soul of another's? If someone is wealthy, famous, intelligent, is their soul more valuable than the soul of a poor, unknown, uneducated child?

With the acceptance of the loving spiritual path through life, sharing our soul's innate wisdom and unconditional love with others, we realize every soul, despite our differences, is equally important. Wealth, prestige, race, ethnicity, genus, matter not. Every person and form of life is intimately linked to each other by a soul, a spirit within. Only together, selflessly helping each other and respecting the lives of all others, may we discover our true purpose in life.

The Source of All Problems

There are some problems in the world, like those caused by nature, that may not be prevented. The source of all of humanity's other problems, however, may be narrowed to just one cause: the ego, our learned beliefs. The ego's purpose is to increase our self-esteem and help us survive in a self-centered world. We are taught success in life is having money, material possessions, and being able to enjoy life's many pleasures. The result of living in such a world is prejudice, inequity, endless wars, hunger, amongst many other needless problems.

Within every life though, is a spirit, a piece of god as well. The spirit's beliefs are almost polar opposite of the ego's, believing every life is equally important. Our spirit wishes to selflessly help others, regardless of our differences, so everyone may succeed and live a life of meaning.

The source of all problems is the acceptance of our learned beliefs, silencing the wisdom and unconditional loving messages of our spirit within. We awaken when we first sense the quiet messages from our spirit, beginning us to question our self-centered views of life. We become enlightened when the spirit becomes the primary guide in our life, understanding much of what we once believed to be true was not. We now realize only when we all succeed together may we truly live a life of genuine meaning and purpose.

The Right Thing To Do

How do we decide what the right thing to do is? For most, it depends on their beliefs, formed when they were young as they learned about the world they live in. Many of their self-centered ideas and prejudices were shaped during these early formative years, often remaining with them for the rest of their lives. During those years we learn to judge others according to their beliefs, ethnicity, race, wealth, or any of hundreds of other ways we differentiate ourselves from each other. This allows us to feel superior to others; at times, since we believe their life is not as important as ours, taking advantage of them to get what we want. This is never the right thing to do.

With the acceptance of the spiritual path through life though, allowing our spirit's wisdom and unconditional love to be our primary guide in life, we realize there is never a reason to hurt another. It matters not if the injury is verbal, physical, emotional, or from ignoring the struggles of those due to prejudice, hunger, poverty. The right thing to do is to always treat everyone, regardless of our differences, with respect, compassion, and unconditional love. Every word, action, and deed must help, never harm another in any way; no one should be ignored in their time of need. Only when we always consider what is best for others, rather than just for ourselves, may we be assured we are doing the right thing.

The Spirit is Everywhere

The spirit is ethereal, otherworldly, within everything. It is a piece of god, the life-giving force that connects all living things. When we allow the spirit, rather than the ego, our self-centered beliefs, to be our primary guide in life, selflessly sharing its wisdom and love with others, we will have learned the lesson we are alive to understand.

Think of the spirit as a star. Everything the rays of the star touch are infused with part of the spirit; this includes water, mountains, the air we breathe, and anything else the rays of light touch. In higher organisms, such as human beings or animals, think of the spirit as two-dimensional. The spirit is within each higher life form as well, there to give our lives direction and meaning. With our death, though our body and ego will perish, the spirit will return to its star, until its rays will reach out into the universe once more.

We are all therefore inextricably linked together by the spirit, a piece of god present within each. Everything touched by the rays of the star has a spirit within, connecting us all to another and to the universe itself. Only together, always respecting the spirit within everything it is a part of, may we discover our true purpose in life.

The Spiritual Evolution of Humanity

We live in a self-centered world dictated by the ego, our learned beliefs. We are taught what to think, how to act, what our prejudices will be. Many therefore go through their entire life concerned only for themselves, rather than other people, life forms, or our planet itself. This is the cause of many of humanity's self-inflicted problems and harmful emotions. Though humanity is rapidly evolving technologically, it is not doing so spiritually.

We awaken when we first sense the quiet messages from our spirit within. These messages are about sharing our wisdom and unconditional love, our spirit, to selflessly help all others in need, regardless of our many differences. The spiritual evolution of humanity will only occur when, instead of blindly following our self-centered views of the world, we allow the spirit, a piece of god present within, inextricably connecting each of us to the other, to be our primary guide in life instead.

We Are All Related

We grow up isolated from each other, thinking we are only related to our immediate family. When we believe that, we tend to distance ourselves from other people. Though we may have a few close friends and many acquaintances, it is the belief our family are our only relatives that further separates us from each other.

In truth, every person, regardless of our differences, is related to each other. For within each is a piece of god, a spirit linking us all together. We are therefore all related by the spirit within each of us, intimately connecting us to the other.

If we take this one step further, consider other forms of life. They too have a spirit, a piece of god within them as well. Therefore, we too are related to everything alive, not only on our planet, but in the universe as well. All life, regardless of our differences or genus, is interconnected, linked, related to each other by a piece of god, a spirit within each, inseparably joined together by a universal bond meant to be selflessly shared with all others.

We Must Change Ourself First

We grow up in a world where we are taught what to believe, including our prejudices and self-centered view of life. Most, therefore, worry only about themselves with little regard for others. Believing there is little they may do to help those in need, they do not even try, ignoring the struggles so many endure.

Before we may change the world though, we must first change ourself. For if we do not, any change in the world will be fleeting, temporary, until those in power decide to undo its benefit. For genuine change to happen we must first gaze within to discover the truth. Within every life is a spirit, a piece of god seeking to share its knowledge, wisdom, and ultimate truth about existence. When we first sense our spirit within, we awaken, questioning our self-centered beliefs about helping others and our purpose in life. As these messages become more prominent, we dedicate the rest of our life to changing the world by helping others understand this as well.

We Live in a World of Possibilities

Though we live in a world of endless possibilities, we are brought up to believe this not true. By accepting everything we are taught, we put limitations on what we may accomplish in the world. We therefore believe our life is predestined: we are born, go to school, get a job, make money, have a family, buy material possessions, and try to enjoy life.

When we do so, we neglect the unlimited possibilities life truly offers, for these may not be found in the self-centered world. Rather, they exist only within each of us, where a spirit, a piece of god accompanies us through our life's journey. Only by following the spiritual path, allowing it to be our primary guide, will we truly understand the unlimited possibilities we may each accomplish. By selflessly sharing our spirit's innate wisdom and unconditional love with others, every one of us has the ability to unlock our potential and in doing so, change the world. All we lack is the sincere belief we may do so.

The Two Paths Through Life

There are but two paths through life. Although it may appear there are many more, there are not. The first is the self-centered path of the ego, our learned beliefs. This path emphasizes what is best for us; it has little concern for others. Simply look at the world today and throughout history to see the results of following this path: endless wars, hunger, climate change; prejudice, greed, inequity, are but a few of humanity's many challenges and problems living in such a world.

The second path through life is that of the spirit. Also known as our higher-self, it symbolizes a piece of god accompanying every life. This path, representing the rhythmic energy of the universe flowing within, emphasizes what is best for everyone.

We each choose which path will guide us. Most follow the path of the ego, believing success in life is making money, buying material possessions, having a family, enjoying the best things life offers. The spirit, however, believes true success in life may not be found in the world. It must first be discovered within by embracing the loving spiritual path, then it must be selflessly shared, without motive or benefit, with all others, so they too may live a successful life as well.

We may change our path through life at any time. We begin to do so when we awaken, starting to question if everything we learned was true. As we realize little of it was and accept the spiritual path instead, an inner peace and feeling of unrelenting love overpowers us, as the genuine meaning of life now becomes evident.

We Are One People

Though we are all unique in appearance, have many diverse beliefs, are we truly different? Believing we are is the cause of prejudice, inequity, endless struggles, and many of humanity's self-inflicted problems and challenges in the world.

With the embrace the spiritual path though, we realize that though we look, act, and believe differently, we are separated only by our self-centered beliefs. With the understanding a spirit dwells within every person, intimately connecting us to each other, we realize we truly are one people, alive to embrace our similarities, not our differences. That rather than being strangers, we are all family, brothers and sisters, in a common journey to understand this.

Look past the façade, beliefs, and appearance of another to understand our commonalities, the spirit within, then selflessly share its unconditional love, knowledge, and wisdom about existence with others. Doing so we will have achieved our life's purpose and learned the lessons we are alive to understand.

What is Love?

Every person and higher form of life seeks love, wishing to intimately share their life with another. Before we find love though, it is important to define it. There are two types of love: learned and inherent. We learn about love as we experience life, wishing to have our love reciprocated by those we truly care about; this is conditional love. Though we may believe it is real, it is often temporary, fleeting, depending on changing circumstances in our life and in the lives of those we share our love with.

Inherent love comes from within. It is shared by our spirit and is freely given without motive or benefit. Spiritual love is a much deeper form of love, coming from our heart, rather than our mind. Only when we understand this, will we be able to find true love in our life and in doing so, discover our life's genuine purpose as well.

Our True Purpose in Life

Within every life is a spirit, a piece of god. Its intention is to push us to explore deeper meanings in life. With our birth though, the ego, our learned beliefs, is created. The ego is self-centered, defining success as money, prestige, material possessions, and being able to enjoy the best things life offers.

Most follow the egoistic path through life. This results in a world of unending wars, hunger, senseless violence; of greed, prejudice, inequity. Though some may succeed in life, the path of the ego will lead to a life lacking purpose or meaning.

The true meaning of life is to embrace the spiritual path, sharing its innate wisdom and love, regardless of our differences, to selflessly help others. The spirit's messages though, are often silenced by our overpowering ego. When they are, we remain asleep. We awaken when the first quiet messages from our spirit are sensed. When we understand our self-centered definition of success is flawed, the spirit becomes our primary guide, beginning us on a quest to discover our true purpose in life.

What is Awakening & Enlightenment?

Within every life there are two competing, often contrary entities: the spirit and the ego. The spirit is a piece of god, the transcendent aspect of human awareness that connects us to something greater than ourself. The ego is everything we learn and accept is true. Its only concern is what is best for us, worrying little about others.

Most follow the path of their dominate self-centered ego, silencing the messages of their spirit within. This results in a world of endless wars, inequity, prejudice, and many of humanity's self-inflicted problems and harmful emotions.

We begin to awaken when the first quiet messages of our spirit are sensed. Though we may be successful in life, we cannot ignore these feelings. They are about improving the life of everyone, even those who are different than us or we may not know, and sharing our spirit's wisdom and love selflessly with all others. Once we awaken, we may never go back to sleep. Everything in our life will change as we begin to challenge all we once believed to be true.

As our spirit's messages become clearer, we begin to understand everything we once believed to be true was not; that the genuine purpose of life has little to do with just our success in the world. Rather, it is to embrace the loving spiritual path, realizing only together by selflessly helping others become successful as well, will we lead a life of true purpose and meaning.

Enlightenment is the complete acceptance of the spiritual path. Though the ego will remain, its influence now will be minimal. This is the lesson we are alive to realize; this is the meaning of life.

What is a Life Worth?

Is one life more valuable than another's? The answer to this question depends on whether we follow the self-centered views of the ego, our learned beliefs, or the loving inherent beliefs of the spirit, present within every life. For those who follow the former, they may view the lives of those who are wealthy, famous, a certain race, ethnicity, or any of hundreds of other differences between us, more valuable than others who are different from them.

Those following the spiritual path though, believing every life is equally important regardless of our differences, do not differentiate the worth of another. There can be no price put on any life. It matters not our beliefs, appearance, wealth, or any other comparison we may make. Every life is precious, invaluable, having a spirit within; each, therefore, has the same exact worth as every other life. The senseless loss of even one life must be mourned, as its spirit will no longer be present to share its infinite wisdom and unconditional love with the world.

We Are More Than Our Labels

As soon as we are born we are immediately labeled. We are black, white, Hispanic, Asian, male, female, Protestant, Hindu. We are categorized in hundreds of different ways throughout our life. Is that who we are? Though these may describe who we are in the world, it has little to do with who we really are.

We are all spirit, each with a piece of god housed within a human body. The spirit is the part of us that transcends time and physical existence. Our appearance, beliefs, or any other differences between us, are not important. We are all the same, intimately linked together by a shared spirit, alive to selflessly help each other in our journey through life.

We are more than who we are identified as. Those who do not believe they are, will never understand the true reason they were born. Only those who challenge this belief, awakening to the possibility they are more than just their labels, may begin a quest to discover their genuine life's purpose.

When You See Another

When you see another person, what do you see? Do you look at their appearance, race, sex? What do you hear? Do you hear what their beliefs are or the true underlying meaning of the words they are saying? Do we judge ourselves by comparing them to us? When we see another, many of us often do all of these things. Some even believe, due to our differences, they are more important than others. This view of the world is the cause of prejudice, envy, inequity, and many of humanity's harmful beliefs and actions.

In spirituality, when we look at another, we see beyond their façade, appearance, and words, to their spirit within. There is no judgement; every life, regardless of our differences, is perfect, equal in every way, each deserving to be treated with respect, compassion, and unconditional love. Only when we gaze past another's outer shell to their spirit within, will we know who they truly are.

When a Child Dies

There are times children die due to severe accidents, illnesses, or in other ways beyond our control. But many children die from preventable causes: war, starvation, or the dangers of living in a violent, insensitive self-centered world. It is inexcusable for any child to die needlessly from something that may be prevented.

Any child's senseless death is a loss to all of humanity. Is one child's life worth more than another's? Is the child of wealthy parents worth more than the child of a poor, minority, immigrant parent struggling to survive? Is a Jewish child's life more valuable than a Palestinian child? Despite our circumstances in life, does not every mother feel the same anguish with the death of her child?

Every child's life, regardless of our many differences, is equally important, each having a spirit, a piece of god within, connecting each child to the universe itself. The senseless death of even one child, along with their loving spirit within, is a loss to all. There is never a reason to accept the death of a single child, for their life's worth is beyond measurement.

Why is it So Hard to Become Enlightened?

Enlightenment is the complete acceptance of the spiritual path through life, understanding every life has a spirit, a piece of god within. The spirit is the life-giving force that connects all living things together. With our birth though, the ego, our self-centered beliefs, is created. With our ego's dominance, we soon forget our purpose in life, as the messages of our spirit are silenced.

There are some who have awoken, sensing the first messages from their spirit within, who may get glimpses of the incredible inner peace and infinite love associated with enlightenment; circumstances in their life though, may abruptly end these feelings. The death of a family member, divorce, loss of a job, or any number of other events may mitigate these blissful emotions. Stressors, bringing back unpleasant memories from the past, may arise as well.

Enlightenment will be only be long-lasting when we whole-heartedly accept the spiritual path, remembering our spirit's original purpose by selflessly sharing its wisdom and unconditional love to benefit all others.

Why?

Why is there greed, prejudice, inequity? Why do we judge other people by their race, ethnicity, religion, wealth, or any of the hundreds of other ways we differentiate ourselves from each other? We do so because of the ego, our self-centered beliefs, as it tries to bolster our self-esteem and justify our actions. We accept war, starvation, prejudice, as simply being part of life. We believe, though we feel these things are wrong, there is little we may do to bring meaningful change, so we pretend it does not happen.

We need not live like this though. Our bodies are simply a shell, housing both our spirit and ego. To change the course of humanity, we need to awaken and adopt the spiritual path as our primary guide through life. Our spirit, present within each life, unites and intimately links us all together. It is only when we selflessly share with others our spirit's unconditional love, knowledge, and wisdom about existence, humanity's problems may begin to mitigate, ridding the world of many of the unanswered questions above in doing so.

How Long Can We Pretend Not to See?

We live in a world of greed, prejudice, inequity, where needless deaths from war, random violence, drugs, occur daily; where hunger, homelessness, poverty, are but three of numerous manmade human challenges causing endless struggles for so many. How long may we pretend not to see? Whether it be seeing the dead bodies of innocents retrieved from bombed out buildings, the ribs of small children protruding from their bodies due to lack of nourishment, or the random violence and drugs destroying the lives of so many.

This need not continue to happen. We have the ability now to effect change, but to do so we must no longer ignore any wrongs or tolerate any injustices. In spirituality, a wrong is anything causing harm to another in any way. It matters not if it is verbal, physical, or through allowing others to go hungry, homeless, or to be treated differently due to their differences. Only by no longer pretending we do not see and adopting the spiritual path through life, may we all encourage genuine in the world, and in doing so, allow humanity to begin its spiritual evolution as well.

A World United

From the moment we are born we are taught to see a world divided by sex, religion, race, ethnicity, wealth, and in hundreds of other ways. Every comparison separates rather than unites us. Divisions are learned and are the cause of many of humanity's prejudices, inequities, and innumerable self-inflicted problems and harmful emotions.

In spirituality, there are no divisions. When we see another, we look beyond their façade, their superficial layers and outer appearance, to their essence, their spirit present within each, intimately connecting their life to ours and all others. In a world united, we would selflessly help each other, allowing us all to live a life of genuine purpose and meaning.

A Slow Awakening

With our birth the ego, our learned beliefs, is created, as our indoctrination into a self-centered world begins. We acquire our values, prejudices, and moral compass, believing everything we are taught, often for the rest of our lives. We therefore believe money, material possessions, enjoying life, will allow us to live a successful meaningful life.

For some, though they may achieve their goals, there may come a time in their life they awaken, sensing the first loving messages from their spirit within. Once this feeling begins, it will never abate until they reevaluate their life choices. Their awakening often starts slowly, reevaluating their job, friendships, beliefs, as those they care about often remain asleep. Money and possessions no longer dictate their future; instead, they now wish to selflessly share their money, excess, and love with others to ease their burdens in life, beginning them on a long, arduous journey to discover their true purpose in life.

A Single Life

What is a single life worth? If we took just the elements of a human body, it is probably worth about one dollar. Is that what a life is worth? Is the life of a wealthy, famous scientist or president of a country worth more than the life of a poor, unknown, homeless child living in a faraway land? There are some who believe the answer to the above questions are yes. They therefore immunize themselves to the inequities causing so many to suffer, ignoring the realities these self-centered beliefs cause.

When we awaken, sensing the first messages from our spirit within, we begin to consider the possibility every life, regardless of our differences, is equally important; that the life of one person, despite their accomplishments, is not more valuable than another's. As the messages of our spirit become more prominent, we understand the needless death of even one single person is a tragedy, their essence, their unconditional love and innate wisdom, no longer present to be shared with the world. It is only together, uniting our spirit with all others, that life will truly have purpose. Apart, though we may be successful, our life will have been led without meaning.

A Meaningful Life

Have you ever wondered why we are alive? If you believe what we are taught, it is to make enough money so we may enjoy the best things life offers. Though we may become successful, achieving all our goals, if we live our life only concerned for ourself, not selflessly sharing our success with others, our journey through life will have been a failure, lived without purpose or consequence.

We need not have money, material possessions, or anything else found in the world to live a meaningful life. Our journey through life will only have purpose if we follow the spiritual path, sharing our spirit's divine wisdom and unconditional love to benefit others.

How long we live does not matter as well. Someone who dies when they are young, without achieving success in the world, though who has embraced the spiritual path before their demise, will lead a far more significant life than those who became successful, though did not share their success to help others.

Human Nature

The majority of the world learn what human nature is, believing to be successful, they must make enough money to allow them to enjoy life. Their concern therefore is only for themselves, rather than others. Consequently, we live in a competitive world, learning we must be tough, take advantage of others, do what we must to achieve our goals. Accepting this view of the world is the cause of endless wars, hunger, poverty; of greed, prejudice, inequity, and many other problems caused by humanity's belief this is its human nature.

Our genuine human nature, however, comes not from the world, but from our spirit within, accompanying every life. We are spiritual beings, alive to share our spirit's inherent wisdom and unconditional love with all others, understanding, only together, selflessly helping each other succeed, will we all live a life of genuine consequence and purpose. Though we once knew this before we were exposed to the chaos of the world, we soon forgot it when we accepted the self-centered beliefs of the world. Remembering it once again, then helping others do so as well, is the reason we are born.

Who is God and Where is Heaven?

There are many different beliefs as to who god is and where heaven exists. There are some who believe heaven is above us, where the souls, the spirits of those who were good go after they die. God, they believe, is a supreme being ruling over both heaven and all life throughout the universe. In spirituality though, it is a bit more complicated than this.

When we die, our body and ego, our learned beliefs, perish. Our spirit, however, is immortal, moving to a higher vibrational plane, joining other spirits in an atmosphere of unconditional love and extraordinary inner peace. It is here heaven exists. Imagine each spirit being contained by an unseen energy field. When these spirits come in contact with each other, the proximity of all spirits touching, uniting as one, may be considered god. God knows only unconditional love; there is no pretense, no ego, in heaven.

Heaven may also be experienced though on earth. With the complete acceptance of the spiritual path, an overwhelming sensation of love and inner peace encompass our entire being. By selflessly sharing our spirit's unconditional love, knowledge, and wisdom with all others, we may experience heaven on earth, allowing us to understand the genuine reason for our life's journey as well.

Spiritual Debt

A spirit, a piece of god accompanies every life, connecting each of us to the vastness of existence. Our spirit's messages, however, are often silenced by the overpowering ego, our self-centered learned beliefs.

Spiritual debt occurs anytime we harm another in any way. It matters not if the injury is verbal, physical, or if it is from ignoring the struggles of others we may be able to help in their time of need.

When we approach death, the ego, which may have dominated many of our life choices, realizing it too will perish when its body does, releases its hold on us. At that time, the spirit becomes our primary reviewer. Every soul we ignored, action we took, word we spoke, harmful in any way to another, will be vividly remembered, as our spiritual debt will now need to be repaid.

We may lessen our debt, however, before this. By awakening, sensing the first messages from our spirit within, then accepting the spiritual path earlier in our life, we may begin to repay our debt before we die. By then spending the rest of our life selflessly sharing our spirit's wisdom and messages of unconditional love to benefit others, our debt will be mitigated and upon our death, we will also have understood the lessons we were alive to learn as well.

The Path to Enlightenment

The path to enlightenment is long, arduous, filled with innumerable barriers and detours. It begins before birth when a spirit, a piece of god, joins a new life. At this point, the new life is enlightened, understanding the meaning of its life's journey will be to share its spirit's divine wisdom and unconditional love to benefit others. With our birth though, the ego, our learned beliefs, is created. Our ego's sole purpose is to build our self-esteem, being worried only about what is best for us, having little concern for others.

Most follow the self-centered path of the ego through life, believing to live a successful meaningful life, they must make enough money to allow them to enjoy the best things life offer. Though they may achieve all their goals, become wealthy, have material possessions, a family, if they did not share their success to benefit others, their life will have been led without purpose or meaning.

There may come a time in our life though, when we begin to sense an uneasy feeling arising from deep within, making us wonder if there may be more to life than success and money. This feeling comes from our spirit, as its first messages begin to penetrate the ego's barriers.

Once we awaken, we may never go back to sleep. Our life will change forever as we reevaluate our beliefs, relationships, and life choices. As the messages of our spirit become clearer, we may also change jobs, accepting less money, wishing now to help others, rather than only being concerned for our own success. With the complete acceptance of the spiritual path, we now realize the reason we are alive is to help each other, without motive or benefit, so everyone, regardless of our differences, may find success in their life as well.

The true irony of life is we are born enlightened, then spend the rest of our lives trying to return to that exact moment of time, before our ego was created, and we were exposed to the chaos and challenges living in a self-centered world would bring.

The World is Broken

Humanity chooses to live in a self-centered competitive world, believing money, and what it will permit them to do, will define success in their life. This belief is the cause of many of their self-inflicted problems and harmful emotions. Caring only about themselves, they treat lower forms of life, each other, and the earth itself with disdain, mindlessly destroying each in their desire to succeed.

Our world is broken. Little will change if we continue to follow the status quo, believing we are not accountable for the many problems and inequities so many suffer. The only way to fix our broken world is for humanity to spiritually evolve, realizing, our planet and every life on it, regardless of our diversity or genus, has a symbiotic relationship with each other, and only together, equally respecting all will we survive. Apart, we are all destined to fail.

The Tribes of Humanity

With our birth many of the tribes of humanity are already chosen for us. We are divided by sex, ethnicity, race, and in many other ways. These divisions, defining us by our differences rather than our similarities, only serve to isolate, rather than unite us. They lead to prejudice, believing some people, due to their appearance or beliefs, are better, more deserving than others. They are also the cause of war, inequity, and many of humanity's other self-inflicted problems as well.

In spirituality, there are no tribes. Every person, *despite* our differences, each having a spirit, a piece of god within, is and has always been equally important, deserving unconditional love and to be selflessly helped in their time of need. Though we each appear, act, believe differently, look past the artificial barriers and façade dividing us to the essence within another. It is there humanity's only genuine tribe exists, intimately connecting each of us to the other, forever joining us in an enduring bond of everlasting love.

The Spectrum of Enlightenment

Imagine a line. On the left side of the line is the ego, our self-centered learned beliefs. On the right side the spirit, our higher-self. The spirit is our life force or chi; it is the energy that animates all living things.

Those who believe everything they were taught is true, on the spectrum of enlightenment, are on the far-left side of the line; those who are enlightened, allowing their spirit to be their primary guide in life, on the far-right side. Though we are born enlightened, with our birth the ego is created, beginning our descent toward the left. Most lie in between the two.

The majority of the world spend most or all of their lives on the left side of the line, believing what they learned about the world is true. Accepting this self-centered view of life is the cause of inequity, prejudice, and many of humanity's beliefs and harmful actions toward each other, lower forms of life, and our planet itself.

Some, during their life, may begin to sense a gnawing feeling within, when the first quiet messages from their spirit are sensed. When this happens they awaken, beginning to question if everything they learned was true. At this time, they start to move to the right, a little closer to the center of the line. The more they realize everything they were taught and believed to be true was not, the further to the right they travel, approaching the line itself.

With the complete acceptance of the spiritual path through life, they cross over the line to the right side, now understanding the true purpose of life is to selflessly share our spirit's wisdom and unconditional love to benefit others. Since the ego will remain in a lesser role, few will actually reach the far side of the right line and become enlightened, it is the journey to get there that is the reason we are alive.

Humanity Must Evolve

Humanity is selflessly helping all others in need, regardless of our differences. There are some who try to help, though their aid is often temporary, fleeting, until the next man-made crisis or conflict creates hardship once more. Unless we change the underlying problem though, this cycle of insanity will continue to repeat itself ad infinitum.

Living in a self-centered world of inequity, where the focus is on the individual, rather than on what is best for everyone, is the source of our inhumanity. There are some who are wealthy, while others live in abject poverty; some who eat well every day, while others go hungry; those who live in mansions, while others are homeless.

We awaken, sensing the first quiet messages from our spirit within, when we begin to understand this is wrong. Humanity has the ability now to grow enough food, build enough shelters, share the resources of our planet equitably, so no one goes hungry, is homeless, or continues to needlessly struggle. What prevents this from happening though, is the greed of the few and the acceptance of the rest that this is a normal part of life.

To resolve the underlying problem, humanity must evolve by accepting the spiritual path through life. Only together may we rid the world of its many inhumane challenges by selflessly sharing our excess and unconditional love, our spirit, with all others, so everyone, not just the few, may live a life without struggle.

What is Important?

What is really important in life? We each would answer this question differently. If we were poor, struggling, simply having enough food to eat, shelter for safety, clothes to protect us from the elements, is what would be important to us. For others who may be wealthy, it may be to buy more material possessions, travel, enjoy the best things life offers. Most of us live in between these two extremes.

The reality though is, once our basic needs for food, water, shelter, and safety are met, we all, regardless of our circumstances in life, desire to experience inner peace, true happiness, discover meaning, and genuine love in our life. Most, trying to find these things in a self-centered world, will never find them there.

One need not have money, material possessions, or a prestigious job, to find them. These things exist only within, where the spirit, our higher-self exists, then they must be selflessly shared to help others find them in their lives as well. With this realization, inner peace, true happiness, and genuine love will enrich our lives, and the genuine meaning of our life's journey will have been understood. Discovering the reason we are born and learning the lessons we are alive to understand is what is really important in life. Everything else is simply a distraction meant to challenge our choices in life.

Every Life is Equally Valuable

We live in a self-centered world of judgement, having opinions about others different from us. Race, ethnicity, religion, sex, wealth, are but a few of hundreds of comparisons we judge others by. Believing the lives of some are more valuable than others due to these differences, result in prejudice, inequity, and the needless struggles of many. Humanity even believes, due to its intelligence, its life is more important than all other forms of life or our planet itself. Nothing could be further from the truth.

Within every life throughout the vast universe is a spirit, a piece of god intimately linking each of us to the other. No one life, therefore, each with a piece of god within, regardless of our differences, accomplishments, or genus, is or ever has better or more important than another's. Only together, recognizing the equal value of every life, may humanity's problems begin to abate, and the spiritual evolution of our species finally begin.

The Lesson We Are Here to Learn

We are taught as we are growing up some people's lives are more important than others due to their race, wealth, ethnicity, or any of hundreds of other comparisons we learn differentiate us from each other.

Within each life though, is a spirit, a piece of god inextricably connecting each of us to the other. Realizing the equal importance of every life, regardless of our differences, accomplishments, or genus, and selflessly sharing our spirit's divine wisdom and unconditional love to help all others is the lesson we are here to learn, the reason for our life's journey.

Every Life is Precious

We live in a world where some think they are more important than others. Due to their wealth, fame, ethnicity, race, or any of the many other differences there are between us, they believe their lives are more valuable than others who are different than them.

In spirituality, every life is equally valuable. There are no distinctions making one life more important than another's. Each life is precious, having a spirit, a piece of god within intimately linking us to each other. Only together, regardless of our differences or circumstances in life, uniting our spirit's as one, will we all succeed and find meaning in our life as well.

Tears of Sorrow

I feel tears of sorrow welling up within me. Sadness for all the preventable man-made destruction, intolerance, and the many harmful emotions and actions caused by humanity's indifference to each other. Living in a self-centered world, we learn we should do what is best for us, rather than to be concerned if our actions may harm another.

It does not have to be like this though. There need not be war, hunger, homelessness; nor prejudice, greed, inequity. These, and all of the other self-inflicted problems and challenges, result from living in a world where concern is only about the individual, rather than on what is best for all.

There is an alternative, though it will require a shift of consciousness, one where the priority of everyone, all life on our planet, and our planet itself, takes precedence over the individual. Only when humanity truly understands this may my tears end, and the world further its spiritual evolution.

Every Person Can Change the World

We live in a world where many often feel overwhelmed by everything, believing there is little they may do to help others. This feeling, fostered by the ego, our self-centered beliefs, is the cause of apathy, feelings of helplessness, causing us to pretend these things are a normal part of life.

Within every life though, there is a spirit, a piece of god connecting each of us to the other. When we selflessly share our spirit's wisdom and unconditional love with others, we may help awaken in them the genuine possibilities life offers. Doing so, their spirit may then help awaken the spirit within another, ad infinitum, helping bring genuine change to the world.

Living in an Insane World

We live in a world in which we accept the senseless death of innocents from war, starvation, random violence, drugs, as a normal part of life. This world is self-centered; its inhabitants are insane, only concerned about themselves.

Humanity has the ability today to end war, hunger, climate change; to mitigate inequity, greed, prejudice. These and all other of humanity's self-inflicted problems and negative emotions result from living in an indifferent world that cares little about its harmful actions toward others.

We may only begin to alleviate our insanity by embracing the spiritual path through life, realizing we are alive to selflessly help, not harm each other, and that regardless of our differences, every life, each with a spirit, a piece of god within, is equally important. We must no longer pretend we do not see. Only then may we not only begin to mitigate humanity's insanity, but discover the path to its spiritual evolution as well.

True Love

We live in a self-centered world, concerned only for what is best for ourselves, rather than others. When we adopt this view of life, we learn what love is through our experiences in life. Though we may believe we have found love, love found in the world is often temporary, fleeting, only present until circumstances in our or another's life may alter its presence.

True love must first be discovered within by embracing the unconditional loving messages of the spirit, then it may only be known by selflessly sharing it with others to help each find true love in their life as well.

Making Real Change

Any change made in the world is fleeting, influenced by those in power and circumstances in life. Though the relief may briefly help others, if it does not address the underlying challenges, the respite will be temporary. Most of humanity's problems revolve around living in a self-centered world, concerned only for ourselves, rather than others.

For genuine change to occur, humanity must first transform itself by embracing our spirit's divine wisdom and unconditional love, then selflessly sharing it with all others. Only then, by recognizing every person's life, regardless of our differences or accomplishments, each with a piece of god within, is equally important, and by equitably sharing the resources on our planet, allowing everyone to find sustenance, shelter, and the basic needs for survival, will enduring change ensue. It will also allow each of us to begin a journey to discover true meaning and purpose in our lives as well.

Love One Another

We live in a world where greed, prejudice, and inequity reign; where people find flaws with others due to their differences. We each have faults and opinions, often caused by the ego, our self-centered beliefs, trying to bolster our self-esteem and protect us from harm. We therefore may hurt another with our words, actions, or deeds.

There is never a reason to harm another though; the injury wounds us as much as it does the person it is directed at. It impairs our spiritual growth, keeping us trapped in an illusionary matrix.

It is important to gaze past the facade others present to their authentic-self, whose universal knowledge and unconditional love is meant to be selflessly shared with the world. When we are each able to see past our failings and the faults of others, to the loving spirit within each other, we will then able to genuinely love one another, helping change the direction and beliefs of the world forever.

The Irony of Life

Within every life is a spirit, a piece of god inextricably connecting each life to the other. Before we are born, we are only spirit. It accompanies every life and is the source of divine wisdom and intuition within us.

The irony of life begins with our first breath, when the ego, our learned beliefs, is created. The ego's only concern is what is best for us; it worries little for others. We therefore believe success in life is to make money, buy material possessions, and be able to do the best things life offers. By accepting this self-centered view of the world, though we may achieve our goals, if we do not share our success with others, we will have lived our life without meaning or purpose.

Genuine meaning may only be found within by selflessly sharing our spirit's wisdom and love with all others. The irony of life is we are born enlightened, knowing this. Our ego is then created, and we adopt its self-centered views and beliefs about the world. Then, we often spend the rest of our life trying to return to the moment before we took our first breath, before the ego was created, when we understood our life's genuine purpose.

The Eyes of a Spirit

Most look at others through the eyes of the ego, their learned self-centered beliefs, judging them by their appearance, ethnicity, race, wealth, and in hundreds of other ways. There are others, though fewer, who see them instead through the eyes of the spirit, a piece of god present within every life, seeing no differences whatsoever. When they see another, they look beyond their façade and outer appearance, to their loving spirit within. For that who we truly are.

With enlightenment and the complete acceptance of the spiritual path, we are able to see beyond the superficial pretense others present to the world, to the genuine person within. When we do, we realize, regardless of our differences, we are each the same: we are spirit, alive to selflessly share its divine wisdom and unconditional love, helping others remember this as well.

Every Person is Beautiful

When we are born we are taught to accept the self-centered beliefs of the world, including what to think, believe, our prejudices, amongst many other things. We therefore learn to judge others, including whether we consider someone's appearance beautiful or not. Judgment though, only serves to divide rather than unite humanity.

With enlightenment and the acceptance of the spiritual path through life, we are able to see beyond the exterior, the outer shell of another, to their essence, the unconditional love residing within each. For it is here the genuine beauty of another truly lies. When we do, we realize every life, regardless of their appearance or differences is, and has always been, beautiful.

The Simple Lesson We Are Here to Learn

When we are first born, the ego, our self-centered learned beliefs, is created. The ego is the source of many of humanity's self-inflicted challenges in life. Within every life though is also a spirit, a piece of god present to guide our life with its inherent wisdom and unconditional love.

Due to the ego's overwhelming dominance in our life, our spirit's messages are often silenced. We awaken when we first sense our spirit within. By selflessly sharing our spirit's wisdom and love with all others, the simple lesson we are alive to learn will be understood.

Finding Happiness, Meaning, and Love

Life appears complicated, challenging, as we each search for happiness, meaning, and love in our life. These things though, may not be found in a self-centered world. Money, material possessions, family, will not allow us to find them. To discover genuine happiness, meaning, and love, they must first be found within, then, to truly experience them, they must be selflessly shared to help others find them in their life as well.

We Are Each Part of a Whole

We are all individuals: we look, act, believe differently. We therefore tend to forget that, though we are each unique, together we are part of a whole. Humanity, being the dominant species on our planet, focuses only on what is best for themselves, concerned little for other forms of life, our planet, or even for each other.

Though we are separate, we each have a symbiotic relationship with the other, intimately linked by a spirit, a piece of god present within each. It matters not our differences or genus. We are all part of a whole. Only together may we all thrive; apart, we are destined to fail.

The Façade

When we are born, a spirit, a piece of god is present within every life, inextricably linking each life to the other. Our spirit's primary purpose is to dissolve separation and experience oneness with all beings.

With our birth, however, the ego, our learned beliefs, is created. The ego's only concern is what is best for us; it worries little for others. To protect us from harm, it may build a facade, a barrier shielding us from pain other people may cause us with their words or actions.

Though our façade protects us, it also hides our genuine self, our spirit, from the world. Many live their entire life hidden behind their protective shell, never truly experiencing life as it was meant to be lived.

When we awaken, sensing the first loving messages from our spirit within, the initial cracks in our barrier begin to form. As the messages of our spirit become clearer and with the complete acceptance of the spiritual path, our facade fades, allowing the true purpose of our life's journey, to selflessly share our spirit's wisdom and love with others, to be understood.

Who Are We?

Throughout millennia, many have tried to define who we are. Philosophers, religious leaders, amongst many others, have searched endlessly throughout the world, trying to answer this question. Most believe their life will be defined by their identity in the world. We are male-female, Buddhist-Hindu, wealthy-poor, Hispanic-Asian, or any of hundreds of other comparisons we learn differentiate us from each other. Is this who we really are though?

In spirituality, there is a realization we may never find who we are in a self-centered world; we are not our labels. Rather we are spirit, a piece of god present within every life, intimately connected to each other. Only by selflessly sharing our spirit's divine wisdom and unconditional love with all others may we finally discover who we truly are and, in doing so, uncover the genuine purpose of our life's journey as well.

We Are But One of Many

After we are born we are taught we are unique, different from others in many ways. As we learn to accept this view of the world, the ego, our self-centered beliefs, is formed. We therefore believe, though we are one of billions on this planet, it is our differences, rather than our similarities, which define us. This self-centered view of the world isolates us from each other and is the cause of many of humanity's problems and challenges. War, hunger, prejudice, inequity, are but a few of the many struggles resulting from endlessly separating ourselves from each other.

To begin to mitigate these problems, we must instead embrace our similarities, rather than our differences, recognizing, though we are one of many, we are each intimately linked together by a spirit, a piece of god present within each of us. And only together, selflessly helping each other, may we all survive and live a life of genuine purpose and meaning.

The Cause of Humanity's Challenges

Before we are born, a spirit, a piece of god is present within every life. Its purpose is to give our lives meaning by guiding us with its inherent wisdom and unconditional love. With our birth, though, the ego, our learned beliefs, is created. Our ego's only concern is to build our self-esteem and assure our success in life; it worries little about others.

For most, the ego dominates their life, silencing the loving messages from their spirit within. This is the underlying source of all of humanity's self-inflicted challenges and problems. It is the cause of war, prejudice, inequity, hunger, resulting from living in a self-centered world in which the ego dominates our views and beliefs about life.

In order to end this cycle of despair, we must change this paradigm, permitting the spirit, rather than the ego, to become our primary guide in life instead. The spirit is equally concerned for all, wishing to selflessly share its wisdom and love to help those in need. Following the spiritual path will not only mitigate many of humanity's problems, but also allow us to discover the genuine purpose of our life's journey as well.

Our Imperfect Self

Within every life is a spirit, a piece of god accompanying each of us through our life's journey. Our spirit's purpose is to dissolve separation and experience oneness with all beings.

Before we are born, knowing only spirit, we are perfect. With our first breath, however, the ego, our learned beliefs, is created. Believing all we are taught, many grow up worrying only about themselves, as they accept the beliefs, prejudices and views of a self-centered world. This results in our imperfect self, as the ego dominates our life journey, silencing the messages from our spirit within. Many of humanity's problems and struggles result from blindly following the beliefs of our imperfect self.

When we awaken, sensing the first quiet messages from our spirit within, we begin to challenge the beliefs of our imperfect self, as we begin on a quest to discover our genuine purpose in life.

Spirituality and Our Emotions

After we are born we learn what emotions are by watching movies, reading books, observing the world. All learned emotions, both positive and negative, are conditional, often shared so we may get something in return.

There is only one genuine emotion: unconditional love, inherent within every life. This emotion emanates from the spirit, a piece of god present to guide our life with its wisdom and unconditional love. This love is meant to be selflessly shared, without motive or benefit, with all others. It matters not if we know another or if they are strangers.

It is often difficult to reveal our genuine emotions due to the protective barriers, the façade we may build to protect us from harm others words or actions may cause us. Only by breaking down our walls though, may we allow our genuine emotions to be shared.

We awaken, when we first sense our spirit's presence within, challenging our learned beliefs and emotions. As our spirit's messages become clearer, our artificial protective shield starts to yield, allowing us to begin to selflessly share our one true emotion, unconditional love, with others, so they too may then share it with those they meet as well.

Where Are the Answers?

As we are growing up we learn what success, happiness, and love are. We are taught to find these things, we must get a good job, make money, have nice material possessions, a family, and do the best things money allows us to do. We believe if we do these things, we will have led a successful life, full of happiness, purpose, and love.

Though we may achieve our goals, there may come a time in our life when we begin to experience an uneasy feeling within. This awakening happens when the first quiet messages from our spirit are sensed, trying to let us know the answers we are seeking to find success, happiness, and love, may not be found in a self-centered world.

They must first be discovered within, where a spirit, a piece of god is present to accompany each life, then, by selflessly sharing its wisdom and unconditional love to help others find success, happiness, and love in their life, we will find each of these in abundance and discover genuine meaning in our life as well.

We Are the Children of the World

We are the children of the world. When we see what is happening on our planet, we do not understand. Why is there war, people needlessly killing each other, rather than peace where everyone lives together in harmony? Why is there prejudice, judging others who look, believe, or act differently than we do; is not every life, regardless of our differences, equally important? Why is there hunger when we have the ability and technology now to feed everyone alive? Why is there inequity with some people having much, while others struggle every day just to survive? Why are the adults ruining our environment, when we have the ability today to use green alternatives to end this senseless destruction? Why do we kill animals for food when we have alternate sources we may use instead of eating meat? When you look into the eyes of an animal, do you not see their soul within? Why do adults accept living in a world of greed, prejudice, and fear, rather than in a world of love, accepting everyone as equal, important, and worthwhile?

Though our elders have chosen to live in such a world, we do not accept their choices. Instead, we, the children of the world, choose to live in a world of unconditional love, rather than hate, allowing all who live on our planet to live in peace and harmony.

One World

We live in an endlessly divided world separated by sex, religion, ethnicity, race, wealth, and in hundreds of other ways. These divisions isolate us from each other. We therefore are only concerned for our own individual needs and desires, even if those may cause harm or needless struggles for others.

Humanity cares only about itself, worrying little about lower forms of life, our planet, or even each other, believing their life is more important than others. They have forgotten we are one world, inextricably linked by a universal spirit, present within every life and, regardless of our differences, accomplishments, or genus, only together, by selflessly sharing our spirit's divine wisdom and unconditional love to help all others, will our planet and all who inhabit it, survive. Apart, as we are now, we will fail.

The Path We Are Meant to Follow

After we are born we learn to worry only about ourselves, rather than others; to accept the self-centered beliefs of the world. We are taught success is having money, material possessions, a family, enjoying life. Though others struggle, we accept this as being a part of life.

This is not the path we are meant to follow. For most, the ego, our learned beliefs, dominates their life choices, silencing the loving messages from their spirit within. This dominance is the cause of many of humanity's self-inflicted problems and challenges.

The spiritual path recognizes within every life, regardless of our differences, accomplishments, or genus, is a spirit, a piece of god, a conduit for divine cosmic energy. By following the guidance of the spirit, our life will have been lived with genuine purpose and meaning. This is the path through life we were always meant to follow.

Finding True Happiness

We all wish to find happiness in our life. After we are born, we learn how we may do so, believing money, material possessions, a family, enjoying life, will allow us to be happy. Happiness, though, found in the world is temporary, fleeting, like the rain and wind with the passing of a storm. Stress, anxiety, tragedy, may mitigate our happiness as we confront challenges in our daily life.

To discover long-lasting happiness, we must first seek it within, where the spirit, our higher-self accompanies every life. By following the spiritual path through life, selflessly sharing its unconditional love, knowledge, and wisdom with others, not only will we discover meaning in our life, but also inner peace and genuine enduring happiness as well.

Our Life's True Purpose

Every person, possessing infinite wisdom and unconditional love from their spirit, a piece of god within each, may teach others about the genuine purpose of our life's journey. It matters not their education, job, wealth, race, religion, or any other differences between us. We each, having a spirit within possess the same knowledge. We are alive to selflessly share our divine wisdom and love with all others. This is our life's true purpose.

Listen Intently

Every day our thoughts continually barrage us. These thoughts often result from our hopes and beliefs formed when we learned how to survive and succeed in a self-centered world. Our wandering thoughts though constantly distract us, never allowing us to hear the spirit's, our higher-self's messages.

In those brief periods, when our mind is quiet and not racing, listen to the silence in between your thoughts. If you listen intently enough, you may hear a quiet message from your spirit within, as it attempts to share its universal knowledge and unconditional love with you. It is then you may finally begin to realize our life's true purpose is to follow the guidance of our spirit within, then selflessly share its wisdom and love to help others understand this as well.

Raising Our Children With Love

After our children are born, wanting them to be safe, we teach them to be fearful, worry about themselves, their safety, and how to survive in the world. When they are young and impressionable, they therefore develop their prejudices, beliefs, and self-centered view of the world, sometimes for the rest of their life. Raising our children to embrace fear results in a world of greed, intolerance, inequity; of endless wars, hunger, homelessness.

We may choose though, to raise our children a different way. Rather than teaching them to live with fear, we may raise them to live their lives with love instead. Though our children must be made aware and concerned for their safety and how to survive in the world, if we teach them to follow the spiritual, rather than the egoistic path through life, they will realize the equal value of every life, regardless of our differences, accomplishments, or genus, learning to treat each with respect, compassion, and unconditional love. They will understand there is a spirit, a piece of god within every life, intimately linking each of us to another, and only, by selflessly helping and valuing each other, may we all survive and discover genuine meaning and purpose in our life as well.

Dehumanizing Others

After we are born, the ego, our learned beliefs, is created. The ego's only concern is what is best for us; it worries little about others. Most, believing what they are taught, follow the ego's self-centered path through life, deeming success in life is getting a good job, making money, having material possessions, a family, and enjoying life's many pleasures.

Many therefore, worrying only about themselves, ignore the plight of others, often dehumanizing those who are struggling or senselessly dying. They may justify these injustices, believing due their race, poverty, religion, or any of hundreds of other differences, their life is not as important or valuable as theirs. Doing so, they dehumanize them, justifying the struggles they endure as simply being a part of life. This results in many of humanity's self-inflicted problems, challenges, and harmful emotions experienced throughout the world.

Alone, though some may succeed in life, if they did not selflessly share their success and excess to help those who are struggling and suffering, their life will have been lived without meaning. Only together, realizing every life, regardless of our many differences, is equally important, will we discover the genuine reason for our life's journey.

The Invisible

There are those in the world who are wealthy, famous, have a prestigious job, who are very visible, believing these distinctions make their life more important and meaningful than others. There are many others though who are invisible, unseen, forgotten. They may be a minority, live in a poor country, or are struggling to survive, hungry, homeless, living in an indifferent uncaring world. When others see them, they briskly walk by as they are ignored, invisible, their pleas for help going unanswered.

In spirituality, every life, regardless of their circumstances or differences, is equally valuable, each with a spirit, a piece of god within, intimately linking each of us to the other. It matters not if we are seen or invisible; each life is, and has always been, equally important. It is only when humanity acknowledges the invisible, selflessly helping them in their time of need, may they begin to spiritually evolve, understanding, their life will only have meaning and purpose when they help the invisible be seen once more.

The Cause of Hate

Every person and form of life has a spirit, a piece of god accompanying them, connecting each of us to the other. The spirit is the part of us that transcends time and physical existence. Before we are born and exposed to the self-centered beliefs of the world, all we know is spirit.

With our birth though, the ego, our self-centered beliefs, is created; its only concern is what is best for us, worrying little for others. Our opinions, prejudices, and views of the world are formed as we learn how to survive and what is expected of us.

All negative emotions, including hate, are learned. They often begin to form when we are young, as we accept everything we are taught about others who are different from us. Hate soon turns into fear, prejudice, anger, and most other harmful emotions, leading to many of humanity's self-inflicted problems.

For our world to change, we must embrace love instead of hate, permitting our spirit, rather than ego, to be the primary guide in our life. Only then may our world start to heal and may humanity begin to spiritually evolve.

How Life is Meant to Be Lived

After we are born, we learn how our life is meant to be lived. We are taught to be successful in life we must get a good job, make money, buy material possessions, have a family, and do the best things life offers. We also acquire our beliefs, prejudices, and ideas as we learn how to survive in a self-centered world. Those who believe this is how life is meant to be lived, though they may achieve their goals, if their success was not shared with others, their life will have been lived without meaning or purpose.

There is another point of view, however, a spiritual one, about how we are meant to live our life. This view believes we are meant to fully embrace and follow the beliefs of the spirit, a piece of god present within each life, intimately linking each of us to the other. The spirit is our life force or chi; it is the energy that animates all living things. By selflessly sharing our chi, our spirit's wisdom and love with others, the reason we are alive, the lesson we are here to learn will have been understood.

Unconditional Love

Before we may talk about unconditional love, we first need to define what conditional love is. Conditional love is learned by watching movies, reading books, and our daily observations from living in a self-centered world. Though we share our love with another, it is often premised with the expectation our love will be returned. Every learned emotion, therefore, including love, is not authentic.

The only real emotion is unconditional love. Within every life is a spirit, a piece of god, our higher-self. Its presence enables us to give and receive love selflessly. This love is freely given without motive, benefit, or expectation of getting anything in return. The love of a mother, regardless of species, for her newborn baby is an example of unconditional love. A mother would willingly, unselfishly, give her life to protect her baby. A homeless person, hungry from lack of nourishment, sharing the little food they have with another who has none, is another example.

When we selflessly share our spirit's wisdom and love with others, we will then truly know what unconditional love is and will discover the genuine meaning for our life's journey as well.

The World We Choose to Live in

From the moment we are born, we are told what is expected of us. We develop our beliefs, opinions, prejudices about the world, as we learn and believe everything we are taught. This results in us living in a self-centered world where war, hunger, prejudice, inequity, and many of humanity's self-inflicted challenges and harmful emotions dominate our daily lives. These beliefs only divide, rather than unite the world, isolating each of us in a bubble, worrying only about ourselves.

There is another way though, we may view the world. Rather than living in a microcosm, separate from each other, we may instead choose to live in one world, where we are all concerned about each other, rather than only ourselves. In this world, we would follow the universal wisdom and unconditional loving beliefs of our spirit within. Our differences would not matter; all would be equally helped and cared for in their time of need.

The spiritual path is the true path through life we were always meant to follow. It is only if we do so, the future for our children, all other forms of life, and our planet itself, may be assured. Apart, continuing to follow the status quo, we are all destined to fail.

A Great Human Being

What makes a person a great human being? Many believe those who are successful, famous, wealthy, a great athlete, have a prestigious job, or anyone else who has accomplished much in their life, are great human beings. If their success, wealth, and fame are not shared with others, then though they may have achieved much in their life, their lives will have been led without meaning or purpose.

In spirituality, there is only one underlying consideration making someone a great human being; it has little to do with success or accomplishments in life. A great human being is someone who shares their spirit's unconditional love, knowledge, and wisdom about existence, without motive or benefit, to selflessly help others be great human beings as well.

Where is Our Humanity?

Humanity is sincerely caring about others without regard to our differences. Living in a self-centered world of inequity, prejudice, hunger, homelessness, one must ask: where is our humanity? Concerned only about ourselves, our humanity is hidden, ignoring the many difficult challenges others needlessly suffer in the world.

We need not continue to live in such an uncaring indifferent world though. By embracing, rather than ignoring our common humanity, selflessly sharing our spirit's divine knowledge and unconditional love, we can truly help those in need. It matters not our differences, recognizing every life is equally important. This is the genuine loving path through life we were always meant to follow. By allowing our spirit, rather than ego, our learned beliefs, to be the primary guide in our life, the lessons we are alive to learn will have been understood.

Inner Peace

Many people are anxious, stressed, struggling to be successful, make money, survive in the world. For them, finding inner peace may happen for a moment in time, until the next challenge in their life presents itself. Though money does make life easier and less stressful, even those who are wealthy struggle to find inner peace, as events from their past and current life challenges may trigger memories abruptly ending the sensation of calm they feel. Inner peace found in a self-centered world is temporary, fleeting, like the wind and rain in a passing storm.

Genuine inner peace may only be found within, where a spirit, a piece of god accompanies every life. The spirit is the transcendent aspect of human awareness that connects us to something greater than ourself. By sharing our spirit's wisdom and love, selflessly helping others in need, we will discover an extraordinary enduring inner peace, having realized the genuine purpose of our life's journey.

Ignoring Our Spirit

A spirit, a piece of god accompanies every life. It is the life-giving force that connects all living things. By following the spiritual path, our life will have been led with genuine purpose and meaning.

With our first breath though, the ego, our learned beliefs, is created. Our ego's purpose is quite contrary to our spirit's. Its only concern is what is best for us; it worries little for others. For most, blindly following self-centered beliefs of their ego, it dominates their life choices. This results in prejudice, inequity, endless wars, hunger; these are but a few of humanity's many self-inflicted challenges and harmful emotions resulting from living in an egoistic world.

By dominating our life, the ego also silences the messages of our spirit within. For some, they never hear these messages at all. Others though, may awaken during their life, sensing the first quiet messages from their spirit within. Once they awaken, they may never go back to sleep, accepting all they once believed to be true.

There are those though, wishing to return to the life they had lived, who decide to try to ignore their spirit. Perhaps their life was going well, or they simply do not want to confront the uneasy feelings arising within. Doing so may cause anxiety, stress, depression, unhappiness, amongst many other things. They therefore may try to work harder, enjoy their life more, take drugs or alcohol to dull these feelings, or find another way to ignore their spirit's messages. Nothing they try though will work; once these feelings begin, they will never abate.

Though they may be successful ignoring their spirit, when they approach death, the ego releases its hold on their life, realizing it too will perish when our body does. At that time, our spirit's messages will be easily understood. We then realize, though we may have led a successful life, had wealth, many material possessions, a family, if that success was not selflessly shared with others, our life was lived without purpose or meaning.

What We Each Seek

When we are born, the ego, our self-centered beliefs, is created. Our ego's purpose is to increase our self-esteem, being only concerned for what is best for us, not others. We therefore grow up believing the meaning of our life's journey is for us to be successful in life, defining success as having money, buying material possessions, a family, and enjoying life's many pleasures.

Everyone has different desires. Many may define success as having a good job, money, family, though others, who are struggling every day, may see success as simply finding enough food to eat, shelter to protect them from the elements, safety from living in an indifferent, uncaring world. Though we all have the same basic needs, our other desires for wealth, material possessions, and everything else are truly secondary.

In spirituality, what we all seek is much simpler to understand. We truly all want one thing: to find the genuine meaning of life, allowing us to experience the intrinsic feelings of inner peace, true happiness, and enduring love. This will only happen when we clearly hear and accept the messages from our spirit, a piece of god present within not only each of us, but every life as well. Our spirit is attempting to share its universal knowledge and unconditional love with us, allowing us to then share it to help others.

Those who awaken, sensing the first messages from their spirit within, may experience these emotions for a brief moment, desperately wishing to do so again. But life's stressors soon mitigate these feelings, as they return to the chaos of their life.

With the total acceptance of the spiritual path though, these emotions will endure; the feelings of inner peace, happiness, and love will remain with us throughout the rest of our life. This is the lesson we are here to learn. This is the one thing we all truly seek.

Success and Happiness

When we are born we are taught how to become successful and be happy living in a self-centered world. Believing what we are told, we think to find success and happiness we must get a good education, job, have a family, material possessions, and make enough money so we may enjoy life's many pleasures. Constantly striving to be successful and happy though is quite stressful and challenging. Even those who have succeeded in life still try to make more money, allowing them to enjoy life even more.

In spirituality, there is a realization nothing listed above is necessary to live a successful happy life. Though we each require food, shelter, and safety, everything else is secondary. Someone who is poor, struggling, from a distant land, may be happier and more successful than another who remains asleep.

We make our own lives more difficult and challenging when we seek what we do not truly need. When we understand this, regardless of our circumstances in life, we allow our spirit's wisdom and unconditional love to guide our life's choices. We will then not only find true success and happiness in our life, but will also discover the genuine purpose for our life's journey as well.

In Unity There is Strength

We are brought up to worry only about ourselves, believing we must prove we are better than others to succeed in life. This self-centered belief causes us to constantly struggle, worrying others competing with us may take the job we want or be more successful than we are.

Most people believe and blindly accept what they were taught. Their egocentric beliefs dominate their view of the world, silencing the messages from their spirit within. Many go through their entire life believing it was meaningful, successful, having achieved all their goals, yet they never heard the messages from their spirit because of their overpowering ego.

The meaning of life, the lesson we are alive to learn, is to embrace our spirit's guiding wisdom and unconditional love, then share it with all others. When we do, we realize only together, united as one, will we all be stronger. Apart, though some may be successful, if they do not willingly, selflessly share their excess and success with others, their life will have been led without meaning or purpose.

Look Behind the Mask

Within every life, a spirit, a piece of god is present to guide us toward spiritual awakening and higher understanding. Following the spirit's guidance, selflessly sharing its wisdom and love with all others, will allow us to live a life of genuine meaning.

When we are born though, the ego, our self-centered beliefs, is created. Our ego's only concern is us. It attempts to build up our self-esteem and protect us from others who may harm us with their words, actions, or deeds. To accomplish this, our ego may create a façade, a mask we cover our face with. This mask hides our authentic self, our spirit within.

For some who remain asleep, the mask covers their entire face, living a superficial life, never able to experience or know the wisdom and loving messages of their spirit within. For others, who may awaken during their life, sensing the first quiet messages from their spirit, though the mask still partially covers their face, they are able to see a little bit more now. As the messages from their spirit become clearer, realizing much of what they learned and once believed to be true was not, their mask is now completely removed, allowing them to fully see and experience life as it was always meant to be.

Changing the World With Kindness

Kindness is being nice to someone else, sincerely caring about them without motive or intention. It is sharing our spirit, a piece of god present within every life, to make another feel better, cared about, and loved. Every word, action, or deed we take, regardless of any provocation, should always be shared with kindness, never out of malice, always arising from our loving heart, rather than from the judgments of our mind.

As we are growing up, some learn to pass judgment on others due to their race, ethnicity, religion, wealth, or in hundreds of other ways, wishing to feel they are better than others who are different from them. Doing so, when they are kind to another, it is often insincere, given with an alternative motive, perhaps wishing for something in return.

Genuine kindness though, comes from our heart, our spirit, selflessly sharing its unconditional love, our kindness with another. When we share our spirit's kindness, it is because we sincerely wish to make someone feel better.

Doing so, we can change the world by awakening the spirit within another; in turn, by awakening their spirit, their spirit may then awaken another's, ad infinitum. By being sincerely kind to one another, we can change the world one person at a time, awakening each to the true possibilities life offers.

Do Not Wait to Say I Love You

Life is very uncertain. Many believe they will live to an old age, though no one truly knows when they will die. An illness, accident, natural disaster, random act of violence, may prematurely end any life before old age approaches. It matters not race, ethnicity, religion, wealth, or any other comparison; these may not prevent one's early demise.

Do not wait until it is too late, until the day you die, to end a conflict or to let another know you love them. Treat every day as your last, showing them your sincere love and gratitude they are a part of your life's journey. Tell them from your heart, your spirit, a piece of god present within every life, of your unconditional love, for that is where genuine love resides.

In spirituality, sharing our spirit's unconditional love is not limited to only our family or those we know well. Rather it is shared with all, even acquaintances or complete strangers we have yet to meet. It matters not our differences, understanding every life, each with a piece of god within, is equally important and must be loved.

By sharing with others our heartfelt love, we are granting them a gift of not only true love, but purpose in their life, as we may reawaken their love within them as well. Doing so, we will each experience an incredible feeling of inner peace and infinite love permeating our very being. When we share our love selflessly, unconditionally with others, we also will understand the genuine purpose of our life's journey as well.

An Existential Question

Why are we alive? This question has been asked for millennia by philosophers, teachers, religious leaders, and many others. Many believe we are alive to go to school, get a well-paying job that will allow us to buy material possessions, have a family, and enjoy life's many pleasures. We believe if we do these things, our life will have been well-lived and meaningful.

Is that why we are alive though; to succeed by achieving all our goals? That is an existential question. In spirituality, there is a belief there is much more to life than just success in the world; that there is a genuine, more important reason for our life's journey, having little to do with what we were taught.

When we understand there is a spirit, a piece of god present within every life, guiding our life with its universal knowledge, the true purpose of life becomes evident: to selflessly share our spirit's wisdom and unconditional love to help all others live a good life and find meaning in their lives as well.

Christ Consciousness

Within every person, there are two competing, quite contrary entities. One is the ego, the other the spirit. The ego is everything we are taught and believe to be true in our life, as we learn how to survive in a self-centered world. Most, accepting all they were taught, choose to live in this world.

Within every life though is a spirit as well; it is a piece of god, our higher-self. Its desire is to help us discover and fulfill our life's purpose. Most, dominated by their egoistic beliefs, do not sense the messages from their spirit within. They therefore go through their entire life believing success in the world will allow their life to be meaningful; it will not.

Most of humanity's self-inflicted problems and harmful emotions are caused by the ego's supremacy. It is the underlying cause of war, hunger, prejudice, inequity, and many other manmade problems resulting from living in a self-centered world.

Christ consciousness begins when instead of the ego dominating our life, our spirit now becomes our primary guide, relegating the ego to a lesser role, as it was always meant to be. With the complete acceptance of the spiritual path through life, realizing, regardless of our differences, only by selflessly sharing our spirit's innate wisdom and love with all others, allowing them to live a successful, meaningful life as well, will we truly understand the genuine purpose of our life's journey.

Christ, Buddha, Muhammad, and others considered prophets, were people who fully understood and embraced this belief. Unlike the ego's interpretation, when Jesus said love everyone, he didn't mean only love those who look, believe, or act, like you. He made no distinctions; he meant love everyone equally, without motive or benefit.

Within each person, just like Jesus, Muhammad, and Buddha, we each have Christ consciousness as well. And we too, just as they, by fully accepting the spiritual path through life, may embrace Christ consciousness in our life as well.

Follow the Path of Your Heart

We each have a choice in life; to live our life predominately following the mind, our learned beliefs, or to primarily embrace the loving beliefs of our heart instead. Those who follow the former, concerned only for themselves, believe success in life is making money, buying material possessions, having a family, and enjoying life's many pleasures. Doing so, they accept the numerous manmade challenges and inequities experienced by many resulting from living in a self-centered world as a normal part of life.

We are each born with a spirit, a piece of god accompanying us through our life's journey. Our spirit's purpose is to encourage our personal growth and evolution. The spirit realizes every life, regardless of our differences or accomplishments in life, is equally valuable, each having a piece of god within linking us to each other, and only together, selflessly helping each other, may we all succeed, find happiness, love, and meaning in our lives. Apart, though some may become successful, if their success was not shared with others, their lives will have been lived without meaning or purpose.

The meaning of life is to follow the path of our heart, rather than the erroneous beliefs of our mind. When we do this, the genuine purpose for our life's journey will become evident and the lessons we are alive to learn will have been understood.

Genuine Change

Many wish for change in their life. Even if they are successful, they often desire more. Genuine change in life though, is temporary, fleeting, lasting only until there are unforeseen changes in our life circumstances. A severe illness, accident, loss of a job, divorce, can instantly undo the change we achieved. The same is true about genuine change in the world. There are some who are altruistic, truly wishing to help others. Change in a self-centered world though is temporary as well, until those in power or something else undoes the desired change once more.

All genuine change must first come from within, where the spirit, a piece of god accompanies every life. By permitting the spirit to guide our life with its universal knowledge and unconditional love, then selflessly sharing it with others, genuine change will not only come into our life, but into the lives of all those we helped as well. When we share our spirit's love and wisdom with another, we may awaken in them their spirit, beginning them on a journey to embrace genuine change in their life as well.

The Absence of Malice

From the moment we are born we are taught what is important in the world. We learn to worry about our success and happiness, with little regard for others. This results is competition, rather than cooperation, further distancing and isolating us from each other. To get ahead, we may need to do, say, or take advantage of others, causing them harm.

Anything hurting another in any way is malice. It matters not if it's by words, actions, or deeds, or if it is from ignoring the struggles of those who are hungry, homeless, alone. It is caused by accepting our self-centered beliefs, not concerned about other's feelings or struggles resulting from the injury we inflicted.

In spirituality, malice does not exist, genuinely wishing only the best for everyone. Understanding there is a spirit, a piece of god present within every life, intimately linking each of us to the other, we realize only by selflessly sharing our spirit's wisdom and truth with each other, will we all succeed, be happy, and live a life of genuine meaning and purpose.

A Well-Lived Life

As we are growing up, we are taught what a well-lived life is. We learn if we make enough money to buy a house, car, other material possessions, have a family, and enjoy the best things life offers, we have lived a good life. Yet there are some people, though successful in life having achieved all their goals, who are unhappy, depressed, unable to find inner peace, true love, or meaning in their life despite their success.

In spirituality, there is a realization a spirit, a piece of god is present within every life, connecting each of us to the other. The spirit is the guiding wisdom and truth within each life. With this understanding, we realize nothing we acquire, experience, or achieve in the world will allow us to live a truly good life.

Though we each need the basic necessities to survive: sustenance, water, safety, and shelter, everything else, including money, material possessions, or anything else found in the world, will not allow us to find what we seek. An impoverished struggling minority child who understands the true purpose of life by sharing their spirit's wisdom and love to help others, will have lived a significantly worthier life than an elderly successful wealthy person.

A well-lived life will only be led when we understand the genuine purpose of life, the lesson we are alive to learn, is to fully embrace the spiritual path, then selflessly help all others, regardless of our differences, be able to live a well-lived life as well.

What We Leave Behind

When we die, what do we leave behind? If we were successful in life, had a lot of money and material possessions, we may leave those to our family or charity. Is that all we leave behind? For when we die, regardless of our success in life, nothing we have will accompany us. We will be buried or cremated just like everyone else, even those who were unknown or struggling.

If we believe what we will leave behind are our accomplishments, though we may have been famous, wealthy, powerful, then we have lived our life without understanding the genuine purpose for which we were born. If our success was not selflessly shared with others, nothing we accomplished during our life will truly define our life's worth. After time, the memory of who we were will eventually fade. And though we may be remembered in history books and by those closest to us, our imprint on others will only be remembered by our achievements in the world, not by who we genuinely were.

In spirituality, there is a realization nothing we accomplish in the world defines who we are. Who we truly are, and have always been, is spirit, a piece of god present to guide us toward spiritual awakening and higher understanding. This is the lesson we are alive to learn. This is who we truly are.

What we leave behind has little to do with wealth, fame, prestige, or anything else we believed would define our lives. What we leave behind is our spirit, continuing to influence others after our death, who we positively affected in their lives by sharing its wisdom and love to selflessly help them in their life's journey. Everything else is simply an illusion we learn to believe after we are born, to deflect our attention from our true purpose in life.

The Janitor and the President: Life Lessons

If we look at two people's lives, a janitor and a president, examine how meaningful their lives are, most would agree a president's life is far more valuable than the life of the janitor. The president may be the leader of a country or head of a large corporation employing many people, who is able to influence others due to their prestigious position. They also may be wealthy, have many material possessions, and the best of everything, whereas the janitor may be unknown and have very little.

If we believe what we are taught, the majority would agree the president's life is far more worthwhile, contributing much more to improving the lives of other people than the janitor. Believing the worth of someone is determined by their prestige, fame, intelligence, wealth, they naturally come to this conclusion.

In spirituality, though, there is a realization everything the president represents, wealth, influence, prestige, fame, has little to do with how worthwhile or important their life is; that the true worth and meaning of a life may not be found in a self-centered world. It may only be discovered within, where a spirit, a piece of god accompanies every life to share its unconditional love, knowledge, and wisdom about existence with others. When we do our life will have been lived with genuine meaning and purpose.

If the janitor genuinely realizes this and the president does not, then the janitor has lived a far more meaningful life than the president of a country or large corporation. Our accomplishments do not define our life, though many believe they do. A janitor, who may empty the trash and mop the floors of the president, may therefore lead a far more significant worthwhile life than a president who does not understand this.

Only Together Will Our Lives Have Meaning

We are born into a self-centered world. We learn if we become famous, wealthy, have a prestigious job, are able to have many material possessions, a family, and enjoy life's many pleasures, then we will have led a meaningful life. Even if we achieve our goals though, if our success is not unselfishly shared with others, so they too may succeed, we have simply deluded ourselves into believing our life had meaning.

In spirituality, there is a realization genuine meaning may never be found in the world or alone. It must first be uncovered within, where a spirit, a piece of god accompanies every life. The spirit is the source of divine wisdom, intuition, and unconditional love within us, allowing us to selflessly share it to improve the lives of all others.

There is an understanding every life, regardless of our differences or accomplishments, is equally important, and only together, by selflessly sharing our spirit's wisdom and love, will our life truly have meaning, and will we discover the genuine purpose of our life's journey as well.

Finding Inner Peace

Before we are born and exposed to the noise, chaos, and beliefs of a self-centered world, we know only inner peace. A spirit, a piece of god is present within each life, there to help us discover and fulfill our life's purpose. It matters not our differences, knowing each, inextricably linked together by a piece of god within, is equally important. Remembering this during our life, we will experience enduring inner peace, unconditional love, and rediscover our life's true purpose.

With our birth though, the ego, our learned beliefs, is created. From that moment in time, most will never experience true inner peace again. Believing inner peace, happiness, and love, will only result if they become successful in the world, they strive to get a good job, and make enough money to have material possessions, a family, and enjoy life's many pleasures.

There are those though, who are wealthy, famous, lacking for little, who are so distraught, they never know inner peace. And others, having very little, who experience inner peace in abundance. Genuine inner peace may never be found in the world; money, material possessions, being with another, will not allow us to experience it. It may only be found within by following the spiritual path through life, selflessly sharing our spirit's universal knowledge and eternal love with others so they too may experience inner peace in their life as well. With this understanding and remembrance of our true purpose in life, we will experience extraordinary inner peace that will forever endure.

Stand and Be Counted

We live in a self-centered world where we are taught to worry only about ourselves, rather than others. We learn we will find success, happiness, and meaning in our life if we get a good job, allowing us to make enough money to buy a house, have a family, and enjoy the best things in life. These beliefs are the cause of many of humanity's self-inflicted problems and harmful emotions.

Humanity was never meant to follow this path through life. Rather, they were always intended to follow the path of the spirit, a piece of god present within each of us, understanding, regardless of our many differences, we are all connected, intimately linked together, and only by sharing our spirit's awareness and unconditional love with each other, may true change come to the world, mitigating many of humanity's self-destructive tendencies.

We must each stand and be counted by following the spiritual path through life, recognizing the equal importance of every life. No longer may we just focus on ourselves and what is best for us. Instead, we must selflessly share our excess and our spirit's wisdom and love with all who are struggling, so they too may find success, happiness, and meaning in their life as well.

The Eyes of Love

Most know only romantic love. This type of love though is often fleeting, depending on changes in relationships, stresses, arguments, amongst many other things. It also may be influenced by the outer appearance or façade of another person.

Though many believe this is what genuine love is, it is not. Within every life is a spirit, a piece of god that enables us to give and receive love, so we may then selflessly share its love, without motive or benefit, with all others. This love is given regardless of our differences, appearance, or even if another is a stranger.

When we look at the world through the eyes of the spirit, it matters not the race, ethnicity, external beauty of another. For every person, when seen through the eyes of unconditional love, is perfect in every way.

Our Most Important Thoughts

When we are born, the ego, our learned beliefs, is created. As we learn to survive in a self-centered world we are taught success in life may only be achieved if we get a good job, make enough money to have nice material possessions, a family, and enjoy life's many pleasures. As we get older and become adults, most of our thoughts, arising from our mind, the ego, therefore revolve around how we may reach our goals.

Though these things are important to us, is that where our most important thoughts come from? In spirituality, there is a realization our most important thoughts do not arise from our mind, but, metaphorically, from our heart, where the spirit, a piece of god, accompanies every life. Our spirit's purpose is to dissolve separation and experience oneness with all beings.

Our most important thoughts do not originate from our mind, but rather come from our heart, our spirit within. Einstein once said he may attempt 200 experiments; 199 of them fail, only one of them may succeed. Why did that one succeed? Perhaps the first 199 attempts arose from his mind, while the successful one came from his heart, as his spirit intervened, sharing its wisdom with him. When Martin Luther King gave his "I have a dream" speech in the early 1960s, did the extraordinary messages of love come from his mind or were they influenced by his spirit within? When Jesus, Mohammed, and Buddha, shared their innate wisdom and extraordinary messages of love, did their ideas arise from their mind or heart? These are but a few examples of many of perhaps the spirit helping influence humanity's destiny.

To discover true meaning in life, listen to your heart, then share its messages, wisdom, and love, to selflessly improve the lives of all others.

The Answers We Seek

What questions must we first ask before we get the answers we seek? We each desire to be successful, most defining success as having money, a family, material possessions, finding love and happiness in the world. We therefore believe the answers to achieving our goals will be to get a good job, fall in love, and enjoy the best things life offers. If we do this, we trust the answers we seek will be revealed to us.

In spirituality though, there is a realization any answers found in the self-centered world will never allow us to truly discover what we seek. Success, happiness, meaning, and love, found in the world is often fleeting, temporary, depending on our current circumstances in life. Stress, divorce, loss of a job, death of someone close to us, or any number of other factors may change our life instantly.

The answers we truly seek must first be discovered within, where a spirit, a piece of god accompanies every life, present to share its knowledge, wisdom, and ultimate truth about existence, so we may then help others find the answers they seek in life as well.

After Enlightenment

Before we are born, a spirit, a piece of god is present within every life, connecting each of us to the other. Our spirit's purpose is to transcend ignorance and reach divine understanding. With our birth though, the ego, our learned beliefs, is created. The more we accept what we are taught, the more dominant our ego becomes, silencing the messages of our spirit within. The majority of the world adopt the self-centered path through life, believing money, material possessions, having a family, will make their life meaningful and successful.

There may come a time in our life though, when we begin to question if what we were taught is true, sensing the first quiet messages from our spirit within. As these messages become clearer, we begin to realize everything we learned about living a meaningful successful life was wrong; it was a myth propagated by our self-serving ego.

Enlightenment is the complete acceptance of the spiritual path, allowing our spirit to become the primary guide in our life. With this understanding we realize, once again, selflessly sharing our spirit's wisdom and love, regardless of our differences, with all others is the genuine purpose of our life's journey, the lesson we are alive to learn.

Something else happens though after we awaken as well. Those closest to us often remain asleep, still embracing life's illusions. We may find we no longer have much in common with them and therefore, may begin to distance ourselves from them as our paths in life diverge. Instead of only wishing to have meaning and success in our life, we now wish to spend the rest of our life helping others to find meaning and success in their life as well.

Behind the Illusion

After we are born we are taught how to survive in a self-centered world. We therefore learn to be concerned only for ourselves, worrying little about others. Some create a façade, a false impression they present to the world. They may be so good at creating this illusion others have no idea that behind their façade is tremendous stress and unbearable pain.

The illusion masks the spirit, our authentic-self present within each life. The spirit is the source of divine wisdom and intuition within us, so we may then share it with others. This is the path through life we were always meant to pursue. Hidden from most by the dominant ego, their learned beliefs, they live their life asleep, believing who they truly are is the façade they present to the world, not the loving spirit within.

The purpose of life, the lesson we are alive to learn, is to awaken, then follow the spiritual path by sharing our spirit's unconditional love, knowledge, and wisdom about existence with the world. This is what is behind the illusion we present to the world. When we truly understand this, our self-centered beliefs no longer block our view of the world, taking the supportive minor role they was always meant to assume. Instead, we now see a world of unlimited possibilities, realizing, regardless of our differences, we are alive to help others see behind their illusion as well.

An Extraordinary Life

What is an extraordinary life? For some, it would mean becoming famous, wealthy, having a prestigious job, enjoying the best things life offers. Is that what truly defines an extraordinary life though?

In spirituality, there is an understanding wealth, material possessions, fame, prestige, or anything else we learned would allow us to live an extraordinary life, is truly not necessary. A poor, uneducated, homeless person living in a distant land may have lived a more exceptional life than another who has accomplished much.

What defines an extraordinary life in spirituality is understanding our genuine purpose in life is to transcend ignorance and reach divine understanding. The more we share our spirit's wisdom and love, the greater our life will have been. Those who have accomplished much in their life, if they did not selflessly share their excess and success to help others, will have lived a very ordinary life, lacking meaning or purpose. Though another, with none of the recognition or excess, who helps others without motive or benefit, will have led a truly extraordinary life and realized their genuine life's purpose as well.

One World Together

When we look at the world what we see are many separate diverse parts, consisting of people, animals, trees, oceans, amongst numerous other unique features on our planet. Since humanity is the dominant species, they believe they are more important than all other forms of life and everything else adorning our beautiful world as well. If we consider only human beings, we further divide ourselves by race, ethnicity, sex, wealth, and in hundreds of other ways. Some even believe, due to our differences, their life is more important than another's.

Many of humanity's vast self-inflicted problems result from seeing the world as separate, divided, rather than seeing our similarities and dependence on each other instead. In spirituality, there is a realization, every life, regardless of our differences or genus, is equally important, intimately linked to each other by a spirit, a piece of god present within each and, only together, selflessly helping each other, may our planet and all life on it, thrive.

We are one world, united, held together by our connection to one another, equally reliant on each other to not only survive, but to discover true meaning and purpose in our lives as well.

See the Light

After we are born, the ego, our learned beliefs, is created. The ego's only concern is for us; it worries little for any others. There is also a spirit, a piece of god, a life-giving force that connects all living things. By following our spirit's direction, we will live a life of genuine meaning and purpose.

Our ego is necessary and will always be a part of our life. It helps us survive and get along with others in the world, though its dominance is also the cause of many of humanity's self-inflicted problems and harmful emotions: war, hunger, homelessness, greed, prejudice, inequity, all result from blindly following the self-centered path of the ego. The ego's supremacy is the cause of darkness, which reveals itself when we harm another in any way.

When we realize we are spirit in a human body, alive to selflessly share our light, our spirit's love and wisdom with all others, we awaken, allowing us to begin to see beyond the darkness. With the complete acceptance of the spiritual path, we realize who we truly are is light, not darkness. This is the lesson we are alive to learn.

Lessons in Life

No one goes through life completely unscathed. Regardless of our circumstances, we all have situations, both good and bad, that present themselves throughout our life. How we react to the experience will determine if we understand the lesson being offered to us. There are many people who blame others when something untoward happens to them. Though there are times when someone says or does something to cause us harm or upset us, if we blame the other person or react in a negative manner, then we will not learn the lesson we are meant to receive. Rather, we will be destined to repeat it until we do.

There is a reason for everything that happens to us. Every interaction we have is a lesson in life. It matters not if it is good or bad, brief or prolonged, verbal or in another manner, if we remain positive, blame no one, we will embrace the opportunity for spiritual growth it provides.

Every situation, experience, and interaction with another, is meant to help us understand our life's purpose. Anytime we find fault with another for any problems that arise in our life, we are missing an opportunity to learn. Only when we accept everything that happens as part of our journey, necessary to advance our spiritual growth, will we be able to discover the spiritual path, awaken, and begin a quest to discover our true purpose in life.

How We View Life

After we are born we are taught what is important, as the ego, our self-centered learned beliefs, is created. Therefore, many believe becoming successful, making money, buying material possessions, having a family, and being able to do the best things life offers, is what is important. For others though, simply trying to survive each day, obtaining the basic necessities for life is the only thing foremost in their mind.

Though some may become wealthy, famous, have a prestigious job, believe their life was important, when death approaches, a very interesting thing happens. The ego, which is formed with our first breath, realizes it too will perish when our body does. It therefore releases its hold on our life at that time. With our dominant ego no longer controlling our life, we are now able to clearly hear the messages from our spirit within, silenced until now by the ego's supremacy.

We finally understand, what we once believed was important, really was not. For with our death, nothing will accompany us; our money, fame, prestige will no longer matter. All that will be left is our fading memory remaining only with those we truly cared about and selflessly helped in our life.

Our spirit's purpose is to share with us its unconditional love, knowledge, and wisdom about existence, so we may then share it to improve the lives of all others. In spirituality, there is a realization this is the only thing that is truly important in life. For this is the meaning of life, the lesson we are alive to learn.

Do not wait until you approach death to make this realization. Begin now, fully embrace the spiritual path, then selflessly share your spirit's wisdom and love to improve the world and the lives of all who inhabit it.

Our True Destiny

Many people have different beliefs as to what their destiny is. Some think they are born to become wealthy, famous, have a prestigious job, a family, amongst many other things, believing if they attain their goals, they will have fulfilled their destiny. In spirituality, though, there is a realization our destiny does not lie in having wealth, material possessions, fame, or anything else that may be found in a self-centered world.

With awakening, sensing the first quiet messages of our spirit within, we begin to question if we should seek a different destiny by pursing an alternate path through life. As our spirit's messages become clearer, we now understand there is only one true destiny: to reunite with our spirit, a piece of god present within each of us, then share our spirit's universal knowledge and unconditional love to improve the lives of all others. The spirit knows no judgment, believing every life, each with a piece of god within, regardless of our differences, accomplishments, or genus, is equally important.

With the complete acceptance of the spiritual path, we now selflessly share our spirit's wisdom and love to help others reach their true destiny as well. Doing so, our life will have been lived with genuine purpose and meaning, and our true destiny will be fulfilled.

Our Fragile Planet

Peering down on our planet from space its pristine appearance, consisting of a mosaic of shapes and colors, may be observed. We cannot differentiate humanity's many differences from each other. It matters not their race, beliefs, ethnicity, wealth; each is indistinguishable from the other. All we see is how fragile our planet below is, surrounded by a thin blue atmosphere providing life to all who inhabit it. If anything happened to this barrier, all life on our planet would cease to exist.

Humanity has chosen to disregard the damage it has caused to our planet. It has polluted our air, water, land, needlessly caused the extinction of lower life forms, senselessly killed each other due to our differences, and brought our planet to the brink of destruction.

In spirituality there is a realization every life is equally important, each having a symbiotic relationship with the other, and only together, respecting every life, regardless of our differences or genus, may our planet and all life on it survive. Apart, as we are now, though our planet may survive, it may no longer be able to support life on its barren surface.

What is Normal?

What is normal? If we observe the world today, we would consider innocents dying needlessly in war, from random violence, drugs, hunger, normal. Treating others with prejudice, indifference, due to their contrasts, normal. Homelessness, poverty, inequity, normal.

In a spiritual world, no one would be ignored. Rather than continuing to live in a self-centered world of greed, everything would be equally shared so all may survive. Those without food would be fed, without shelter would be housed, in need of help, would be aided.

To change the world, we must all challenge humanity's definition of normal, realizing anything harming another in any way is not normal, and only together, selflessly helping each other, may our world survive, and humanity's spiritual evolution truly begin.

Sharing

When our children are born we tell them they should share their toys with others. The idea of sharing though is not something humanity readily accepts. We live in a self-centered world, concerned only for what is best for ourself, rather than others; we therefore are very reluctant to share anything we have.

When we awaken, sensing the first quiet messages of our spirit within, we begin to question our choices and beliefs in life. We start to realize it is necessary we share our excess with others, recognizing every life, regardless of our differences, is equally important and must be helped in their time of need.

Humanity has the ability now to grow enough food to feed the hungry, to build enough shelters for the homeless, to help all who are struggling to survive in an indifferent world. To do so though, will require us to sincerely care about each other and equally share the resources on our planet. Only together may humanity survive and flourish. Apart, continuing to live in a world of greed, fear, and indifference, we are destined to fail.

Decisions in Life

We each make many decisions every day. Most decisions we make are made to benefit ourselves. When we interact with others, very often it is because we want something in return. Therefore, what is best for us takes precedence over what is best for others.

In a spiritual sense, decisions are much simpler to understand; anything harming another in any way should not be considered. Every decision we make, word we speak, action we take, must be done with the understanding it will not hurt another. Our decisions therefore must always be thoughtfully chosen with love, rather than malice. Doing so, we will awaken, beginning us on a journey to discover our life's true potential.

Our Choices in Life

We may each choose to live our life with fear, accepting the world as it is, or with love, sharing our spirit's unconditional love with all others. When we live our life in fear, we worry only about ourselves. When we live our life with love, however, we are equally concerned for all others as well.

We may change the direction of our life at any time. This may begin to happen when we first sense a presence coming from within. This presence is our spirit, a piece of god accompanying every life, awakening us to the genuine possibilities life offers. This moment in time will alter the course of the rest of our life, as we begin to understand and embrace the spirit's messages to benefit all.

Genuine Love

We live in a self-centered world, concerned only with what is best for ourselves, rather than others. When we adopt this view of the world, we learn what love is through movies, books, and our experiences in life. This type of love though is often conditional, given with the expectation we will receive something in return.

Love found in the world though is temporary, fostered by the ego, our learned beliefs. Changing circumstances in our lives may alter this euphoric feeling, as we deal with life's daily challenges.

Genuine love may not found in the world. It must first be discovered within, by embracing the unconditional loving messages of our spirit, then will only be known when it is selflessly shared, without motive or benefit, to aid others find genuine love in their life as well.

The Value of a Life

How much is a life worth? The elements of a human body are worth about one dollar. Is that what a life is worth? Is one life more valuable than another's? Is the life of someone wealthy, famous, has a prestigious job, worth more than the life of a homeless child living in a poor country? These are questions we must each answer ourself. Many believe some lives are more valuable, judging others by their race, ethnicity, religion, wealth, and in hundreds of other ways.

In spirituality, every life, regardless of our differences, beliefs, or accomplishments, is worth exactly the same as another's. Our true worth is not found in the world. It may only be discovered within, where the spirit is awaiting our permission to selflessly share its universal knowledge and unconditional love to help others realize their true worth in life as well.

What Defines Us?

When we are born we are immediately labeled. We are black-white, Hispanic-Asian, male-female, Buddhist-Hindu, amongst hundreds of other comparisons. As we go through life, the labels of who we are increase. We are a husband-wife, wealthy-poor, doctor-janitor. Is that who we really are? Though these labels describe us in the world, they do not define who we truly are.

We are spirit, a piece of god contained within a human body, accompanying every life. Our spirit's purpose is to transcend ignorance and reach divine understanding. By following the spiritual path through life, selflessly sharing our spirit's wisdom and love to help others find meaning and purpose in their lives as well, we will have learned the lesson we were born to understand.

We are the Source of Our Own Problems

After we are born, the ego, our learned beliefs, is created. Our ego's only concern is us; it worries little about others. It teaches us what success is and how to survive in a self-centered world. Since we are young, many adopt these beliefs, often for the remainder of their life.

We are taught to be successful, we must get a good job, make enough money to live a comfortable life, allowing us to enjoy life's many pleasures. We therefore spend our life striving to accomplish these things. This is the source of all of our underlying problems, believing success and meaning may be found in the world; they will not.

The source of all of our problems is believing success, happiness, and meaning coincides with our job, money, material possessions, family, enjoying our life. Though we may get what we wish, achieving all of our goals, we will not find our answers from any of these things. We therefore spend our entire life searching the world, never able to find what we each truly seek.

Once we awaken, sensing the first quiet messages from our spirit within, we begin to question all we were taught. As the messages of our spirit become clearer, we realize the source of all of humanity's problems result from blindly accepting their self-centered beliefs and only by selflessly helping others find success, happiness, and meaning in their lives, will we truly be able to find these in our life as well.

A Good Person

In spirituality, there is only one definition of a good person. A good person is someone who shares their spirit's eternal love with all others, selflessly helping each in their time of need. They will never say, do, or harm anyone in any way. There are never alternative motives.

They need not receive accolades from others or tell anyone what they are doing. They simply share their goodness, their unconditional love with all others, so their lives may be easier and more meaningful.

We Are All Connected

We are all connected, inextricably linked by a spirit, a piece of god present within each. The spirit's desire is to help us discover and fulfill our life's purpose.

It matters not our differences, accomplishments, or genus. Only together, by merging our spirit's essence with the spirit within others, will humanity evolve and begin a quest to discover the genuine purpose of their life's journey.

The Genuine Meaning of Life

The genuine meaning of life is to fully embrace the spirit, a piece of god present within each of us, then selflessly share its unconditional love, knowledge, and wisdom about existence with all others.

The spirit intimately links each life to the other and only together may we all succeed and live a life of meaning and purpose. Apart, regardless of our accomplishments or success in life, we are destined to know neither.

There Are No Strangers

We live in a world believing family are only those closest to us, related by DNA. Everyone else, besides friends and acquaintances, are strangers we do not know. In Hawaii, there is beautiful word for family, ohana. Ohana means not only family related by DNA, but close friends, neighbors, acquaintances, and even strangers as well. Everyone, regardless of their differences or if they are unknown to us, are family.

In spirituality, there are no strangers. We are all related, intimately linked by a universal spirit, a piece of god within. Only when we awaken and truly understand this, the genuine purpose and meaning of our life's journey may be realized: to selflessly help all others in need. This includes not only those we know, but all those different from us or who we may not yet have met.

We are all ohana. We are all family. We are all one.

The End of My Story

We all have hopes and dreams for our future. We learn we will have lived a successful life if we make money, allowing us to have a family, buy material possessions, and do the best things life has to offer. When the end of our story finally arrives though, our body will be cremated or buried; nothing we have will accompany us. The ego, our learned beliefs, will perish as well. Though we may remain in the hearts of those closest to us, our family and a few good friends, that will be the end of our story.

It need not be the end though. For within every life, in addition to the ego, is a spirit, a piece of god present to give our lives meaning. By selflessly sharing its essence with others, part of our spirit will merge with theirs. Therefore, when our body along with the ego dies, our spirit will continue to live on not only in our family's hearts, but within every person we shared our innate wisdom and love with as well. Our life's influence will therefore not end when we die, though will continue eternally to transform the world as part of the spirit of all those we selflessly helped during our life as well.

Author's Note:

It is my hope your understanding of awakening, enlightenment, and spirituality has been enhanced by reading book 1 of '*Our Search for Meaning*'. If it has, could you please take a few minutes to: "Write a Review" and recommend this book on social media and to your friends and family.

Our Search for Meaning was written to try to awaken and help others who are awakened more fully understand what enlightenment is, so their spiritual journey through life may be more fully realized.

Thank you for taking the time to read:

'*Our Search for Meaning*' – *Book 1.* Please consider reading the other two books in this series as well.

Books by Ken Luball

The four Spiritual books in *The Awakening Tetralogy*:
Today I Am Going to Die: Choices in Life
The Spirit Guide: Journey Through Life
Tranquility: A Village of Hope
The Illusion of Happiness: Choosing Love Over Fear

■■

A Mystical Trilogy. '*Our Search for Meaning*' - a series of three books of thoughtful easily understandable spiritual reflections about awakening, enlightenment, spirituality, & the meaning of life.

****

A Spiritual Duology: '*Spiritual Reflections*' - Two books of spiritual reflections using metaphor, imagery, and spiritual insight to explore themes of awakening, enlightenment, and the human pursuit of meaning.

■■

The first three stories in *The Awakening Tetralogy* are written in the first person, following the spiritual journey through life of a child, as they learn the lessons needed during their life to awaken and become enlightened. These books are written in an understandable, interesting, unique narrative, which is both thought-provoking and engaging.

To find links for each of these nine books **please visit my** website: kenluball.com.

About Ken

Peace, Love, & Light

∎∎

My name is Ken Luball ~ Spiritual ~ Seeker ~ Author ~
Guide ~

****

Ever since I was a young child, I knew my purpose in life; it was for me to awaken, find enlightenment, and share my experience and knowledge with others. To reach those lofty aspirations though, I first had to navigate through quite a few unexpected detours in my life. Though I was brought up in a religious family, it did not help me hear the messages from my spirit guide, Bodhi. If anything, religion only further isolated me, teaching me to accept the ego's view of religion rather than Bodhi's. It was not until after I stopped following a formal religion, I finally was able to embrace spirituality, and with this embrace, I awoke.

Spirituality is the belief there is a piece of god, a spirit, within everything that has life, and, because of this, all life is important, equal, and connected. After I awoke, no longer having the dogma of religion handicapping my views, I was suddenly free to explore this philosophy of life more deeply. Only then did I become aware of the mask I wore and the impenetrable wall I had erected around my heart; the mask and wall allowed me to survive in the world. I would always smile, appear happy, though I would often feel intense anxiety within. This was something I never really understood until the moment I confronted my ego. Little did I know these survival mechanisms would have a profound effect on me for the majority of my life. By protecting me from emotional pain, they also isolated me from my family, everyone else in my life, and even from myself. No one could hurt me because I did not allow anyone to get close enough to do so. In turn, no one could love me or was I able to truly love another either. This superficial life, one devoid of risk or pain, left me alone in a sea of people.

It took many years before the first cracks in my wall formed and before I could loosen the mask I constantly wore. It took me almost an entire lifetime to awaken and begin my journey toward enlightenment.

After I was clearly able to hear my spirit guide, Bodhi, I realized everything I had learned from my ego throughout my life was untrue. I had looked for love and happiness in the job I had, the money I made, things I owned, and through my wife and children. With the exception of the latter, I finally realized none of those things truly mattered. This does not mean I am ungrateful to my ego, however. It taught me coping skills and allowed me to succeed, or at least what I thought success was. Though my ego still remains with me, it has taken a more secondary role in my life now, relinquishing its former primary role to my spirit guide, Bodhi.

Decisions were now required. While it was tempting to take this newly found state of being, withdraw from society and all the hate, fear, cruelty, poverty, and greed that plagues it, I knew within myself, this knowledge was to be shared with others. That is my destiny. Therefore, I have written A Mystical Trilogy: 'Our Search for Meaning': a series of three books of thoughtful easily understandable spiritual reflections about life; A Spiritual Duology: 'Spiritual Reflections': two books of spiritual reflections using metaphor, imagery, and spiritual insight to explore themes of awakening, enlightenment, and the human pursuit of meaning; and The Awakening Tetralogy: the first three stories in The Awakening Tetralogy follow the spiritual journey through life of a child, as they learn the lessons needed during their life to awaken and become enlightened. It is my hope you will read these books, and in doing so, begin a new adventure; one where you will awaken and further your journey toward enlightenment with your spirit within.

I do not know if these books will be widely read in my lifetime, though I hope one day they may help others awaken and find enlightenment as well.

"We are all on a spiritual journey of love & peace;
together may we spread light throughout the world."

To read more of Ken's life-changing reflections visit his website:
kenluball.com

Appendix: Our Search for Meaning ~ 1

Glossary......p.3

Prologue: Our Search for Meaning......p.5

1) Who We Truly Are......p.7

2) Why Are We Alive?......p.8

3) How Much is a Life Worth?......p.9

4) Mid-Life Crisis......p10

5) The End of Life......p.11

6) Behind the Veil......p.12

7) A Warning for Humanity......p.13

8) The Human Mosaic......p.14

9) The Path to Spirituality......p.15

10) Listen to the Silence......p.16

11) The Dream......p.17

12) Waking Up is Hard To Do......p.18

13) Imagine God is a Star......p.20

14) The Spiritual Journey......p.21

15) Our Human Limitations......p.22

16) Open Your Eyes...... p.23

17) We Are Born Enlightened......p.24

18) What is Spirituality?......p.25

19) We Are All Ohana (Family)......p.26

20) A Long and Winding Road......p.27

21) What is a Spiritual Awakening?......p.28

22) Life's Illusions......p.29

23) The Spirit and the Ego......p.30

24) The Three Stages of Enlightenment......p.31

25) The Tree of Life......p.32

26) Many Paths, One Destination......p.34

27) The Root of All Problems......p.35

28) Humanity's Arrogance......p.36

29) When Death Approaches......p.37

30) We Are Immortal......p.39

31) A Total Eclipse of the Sun......p.40

32) There Are Only Two Paths Through Life......p.42

33) Are Animals Sentient?......p.43

34) The Appearance of Meaning......p.44

35) With Awakening Everything Changes......p.45

36) Is It Too Late to Change the World?......p.46

37) The Illusion of Happiness......p.47

38) Choosing Love Over Fear......p.48

39) What Happens After You Awaken?......p.49

40) We Are Stronger Together......p.50

41) Our True Path in Life......p.51

42) Spiritual Karma......p.52

43) What is a Successful Life?......p.53

44) What are the Lessons We are Alive to Learn?......p.54

45) The Four Dimensions of the Spirit......p.55

46) We Must Open Our Eyes......p.56

47) See Beyond Our Labels and Façade......p.57

48) Is There More to Life?......p.58

49) How Many More?......p.59

50) What is the Spirit and What is Spirituality?......p.60

51) Unpacking Our Baggage in Life......p.62

52) The Paradox of Life......p.63

53) The World in Which We Live......p.64

54) A Divided World......p.65

55) We are All Children of the World......p.66

56) We Are Not Alone......p.67

57) Humanity's Hubris......p.68

58) The Reason We Are Alive......p.69

59) The Power of Spirituality......p.70

60) The False Path......p.71

61) The Door......p.72

62) Spirituality and the First Five Years of Life......p.73

63) Sleep Well My Child......p.74

64) The Evolution of Humanity......p.75

65) Rasing Our Frequency......p.76

66) Our Spirit is Immortal......p.77

67) Living in a Spiritual World......p.78

68) Our Solitary Journey Through Life......p.79

69) Our Footprint in Life......p.80

70) The Arc of Life......p.81

71) Nature vs. Nurture......p.82

72) Living in the Shadows......p.83

73) Look at Your Reflection......p.84

74) Living a Happy Life......p.85

75) The Path Back to Enlightenment......p.86

76) Is Death the End?......p.87

77) Human Rights......p.88

78) Living a Life of Meaning......p.89

79) The Bus: A Journey Through Life......p.90

80) Is One Life More Important Than Another's?......p.92

81) Tears in Heaven......p.93

82) The Wall......p.94

83) The Struggle......p.95

84) Open Your Heart......p.96

85) A Good Life......p.97

86) The Loss of Innocence......p.98

87) Always Do the Right Thing......p.99

88) The Human Condition......p.100

89) Divisions in Life......p.101

90) Our Genuine Purpose......p.102

91) An Echo Within......p.103

92) Choices in Life......p.104

93) A World Without Boundaries......p.105

94) Forgiveness......p.106

95) Blaming Others......p.107

96) Areas of Grey......p.108

97) A Spiritual Evolution......p.109

98) Between Life and Death......p.110

99) Everything We Learn in Life is an Illusion p.111

100)   The Untouchables......p.112

101)   Enduring Inner Peace......p.113

102)   Helping Each Other......p.114

103)   Heaven and Hell......p.115

104)   Every Injustice Must Be Challenged......p.116

105)   See the World Through a Different Lens......p.117

106)   To Truly Know Another......p.118

107)   Our Only Genuine Emotion......p.119

108)   Living a Good Life......p.120

109)   Live Your Life With Love......p.121

110)   Ego, Spirit, Awakening & Enlightenment......p.122

111)   Spirituality and the Law......p.124

112)   Inhumanity......p.125

113)   In Another Life......p.126

114)   Heartlessness......p.127

115)   Living in an Egoistic World......p.128

116)   Are We Better?......p.129

117)   Living a Successful Life......p.130

118)   Look Into My Eyes......p.131

119)   Living in Peace......p.132

120)   Love......p.133

121)   Looking for Meaning......p.134

122)   Look Past Our Differences......p.135

123)   One Life......p.136

124)   Never Hurt Another......p.137

125)   My Spirit Weeps......p.138

126)   Seeing the World With Love......p.139

127)   Our Barriers......p.140

128)   Struggles in Life......p.141

129)   The Cult of Humanity......p.142

130)   The Circle of Life......p.143

131)   The Gift of Life......p.144

132)   The Future of Humanity......p.145

133)   The Flag of Humanity......p.146

134)   The Eyes We See the World Through......p.147

135)   Stress......p.148

136)   The Great Illusion......p.149

137)   The Soul.......p.150

138)   The Source of All Problems......p.151

139)   The Right Thing to Do......p.152

140)   The Spirit is Everywhere......p.153

141)   The Spiritual Evolution of Humanity......p.154

142)   We Are All Related......p.155

143)   We Must Change Ourself First......p.156

144)   We Live in a World of Possibilities......p.157

145)   The Two Paths Through Life......p.158

146)   We Are One People......p.159

147)   What is Love?......p.160

148)   Our True Purpose in Life......p.161

149)   What is Awakening & Enlightenment?......p.162

150)   What is a Life Worth?......p.163

151)   We Are More Than Our Labels......p.164

152)   When You See Another......p.165

153)   When a Child Dies......p.166

154)   Why is it So Hard to Become Enlightened?......p.167

155)   Why?......p.168

156)   How Long Can We Pretend Not to See?......p.169

157)   A World United......p.170

158)   A Slow Awakening......p.171

159)   A Single Life......p.172

160)   A Meaningful Life......p.173

161)   Human Nature......p.174

162)   Who is God and Where is Heaven?......p.175

163)   Spiritual Debt......p.176

164)   The Path to Enlightenment......p.177

165)   The World is Broken......p.179

166)   The Tribes of Humanity......p.180

167)   The Spectrum of Enlightenment......p.181

168)   Humanity Must Evolve......p.183

169)   What is Important?......p.184

170)   Every Life is Equally Important......p.185

171)   The Lesson We Are Here to Learn......p.186

172)   Every Life is Precious......p.187

173)   Tears of Sorrow......p.188

174)   Every Person Can Change the World......p.189

175)   Living in an Insane World......p.190

176)   True Love......p.191

177)   Making Real Change......p.192

178)   Love One Another......p.193

179)   The Irony of Life......p.194

180)   The Eyes of a Spirit......p.195

181)   Every Person is Beautiful......p.196

182)   The Simple Lesson We Are Here to Learn......p.197

183)   Finding Happiness, Meaning, and Love......p.198

184)   We Are Each Part of a Whole......p.199

185)   The Façade......p.200

186)   Who Are We?......p.201

187)   We Are But One of Many......p.202

188)   The Cause of Humanity's Challenges......p.203

189)   Our Imperfect Self......p.204

190)   Spirituality and Our Emotions......p.205

191)   Where Are the Answers?......p.206

192)   We Are the Children of the World......p.207

193)   One World......p.208

194)   The Path We Are Meant to Follow......p.209

195)   Finding True Happiness......p.210

196)   Our Life's True Purpose......p.211

197)   Listen Intently......p.212

198)   Rasing Our Children With Love......p.213

199)   Dehumanizing Others......p.214

200)   The Invisible......p.215

201)   The Cause of Hate......p.216

202)   How Life is Meant to Be Lived......p.217

203)   Unconditional Love......p.218

204)   The World We Choose to Live in......p.219

205)   A Great Human Being......p.220

206)   Where is Our Humanity?......p.221

207)   Inner Peace......p.222

208)   Ignoring Our Spirit.....p.223

209)   What We Each Seek......p.225

210)   Success and Happiness......p.227

211)   In Unity There is Strength......p.228

212)   Look Behind the Mask......p.229

213)   Changing the World With Kindness......p.230

214)   Do Not Wait to Say I Love You......p.231

215)   An Existential Question......p.232

216)   Christ Consciousness......p.233

217)   Follow the Path of Your Heart......p.235

218)   Genine Change......p.236

219)   The Absence of Malice......p.237

220)   A Well-Lived Life......p.238

221)   What We Leave Behind......p.239

222)   The Janitor and the President: Life Lessons......p.240

223)   Only Together Will Our Lives Have Meaning...p.242

224)   Finding Inner Peace......p.243

225)   Stand and Be Counted......p.244

226)   The Eyes of Love......p.245

227)   Our Most Important Thoughts......p.246

228)   The Answers We Seek......p.248

229)   After Enlightenment......p.249

230)   Behind the Illusion......p.251

231)   An Extraordinary Life......p.252

232)   One World Together......p.253

233)   See the Light......p.254

234)   Lessons in Life......p.255

235)   How We View Life......p.256

236)   Our True Destiny......p.258

237)   Our Fragile Planet......p.259

238)   What is Normal?......p.260

239)   Sharing......p.261

240)   Decisions in Life......p.262

241)   Our Choices in Life......p.263

242)   Genuine Love......p.264

243)   The Value of a Life......p.265

244)   What Defines Us?......p.266

245)   We Are the Source of Our Own Problems......p.267

246)   A Good Person......p.268

247)   We Are All Connected......p.269

248)   The Genuine Meaning of Life......p.270

249)   There Are No Strangers......p.271

250)   The End of My Story......p.272